YOU
AND
YOUR
SPIRITUAL
GIFTS

Kenneth O. Gangel

MOODY PRESS
CHICAGO

© 1975 by
THE MOODY BIBLE INSTITUTE
OF CHICAGO
All rights reserved

Third Printing, 1977

This book was compiled from a series of articles on spiritual gifts which appeared in *The Standard*, volume 63, no. 8 through volume 64, no. 8 (May 15, 1973—April 15, 1964). Permission to reprint was granted by the Baptist General Conference.

ISBN: 0-8024-9821-3

The use of selected references from various versions of the Bible in this publication does not necessarily imply publisher endorsement of the versions in their entirety.

Printed in the United States of America

CONTENTS

FOREWORD

THE RECOVERY of long-lost truth is as exciting and rewarding as the discovery of buried treasure. It even precipitates a gold rush of sorts, with many rushing to mount a caravan to the field of discovery and others taking off helter-skelter, hoping with a minimum of equipment to cadge a nugget or two before the riches are gone.

But, as in all the gold rushes of history, only a fortunate few ever strike it rich. Usually they are the early comers or those who ignore the surface riches and seek steadily for the mother lode until they find it.

The whole subject of spiritual gifts is the lost treasure of nineteenth- and twentieth-century Christianity. The Church has been impoverished beyond belief by the prevailing ignorance of the existence of these spiritual riches. But now the long-buried truth is coming to light again. Widespread excitement has possessed the churches, and the tide of interest in the subject is running at full flow.

Dr. Kenneth Gangel has provided in this book some splendid examples of careful and profitable mining techniques. He pursues the mother-lodes of Romans 12, 1 Corinthians 12, and other passages with productive skill and exposes the glowing truth to be found in each. He is especially helpful in giving practical ways to recognize personal spiritual gifts and in distinguishing between the real and the fool's gold which abounds today.

I commend this book to all who desire to enrich their lives by discovering all that God the Holy Spirit has buried in the hidden lodes of their lives in His sovereign distribution of the spiritual gifts.

RAY C. STEDMAN

FOREWORD

INTRODUCTION

FEW SUBJECTS have received as much attention among evangelical Christians in recent years as the issue of spiritual gifts. One would think that with all this discussion many helpful items would also be in print, but he would be mistaken. Actually there are very few journal or magazine articles, and even fewer books, about the role of spiritual gifts in the contemporary Church.

There are at least two visible reasons for this literary vacuum. First of all, the subject is rather controversial, and one can change his viewpoints faster and more frequently if he does not submit them to the printed page. A more pressing issue, however, is the temptation to gravitate to the more controversial gifts in order to become a part of the hot debate. You will thus find that articles and books on tongues are available in abundant supply. In this book I will deal with the matter of tongues too, but only because this gift appears as one among many.

The broad purpose of this book is to explore the nature and use of *all* the spiritual gifts as they are described in the New Testament. In my opinion, we have neglected many helpful and constructive aspects of the doctrine of gifts while pursuing the more contentious headlines of today. So let's dig into some crucial questions.

WHAT IS THE NEW TESTAMENT WORD FOR "SPIRITUAL GIFT"?

It is unfortunate that neopentecostal influences have become known as the "charismatic movement." In applying this term in such a way, we have allowed one segment of theology to preempt a very important part of New Testament truth. The word *charisma* or *charismaton* is the Greek term which refers to a spiritual gift. The word appears seventeen times in the New Testament, with an approximate grouping into three separate ideas: *God's gift of salvation* (Ro 5:15-16; 6:23); *a general gift of grace or love* (Ro 1:11; 2 Co 1:11; 7:7); *a specific endowment of spiritual ability for service* (Ro 11:29; 12:6; 1 Co 1:7; 12:4, 9, 28, 30, 31; 1 Ti 4:14; 2 Ti 1:6; 1 Pe 4:10).

It is obvious that the third usage is prominent and that the central passage is 1 Corinthians 12. Apart from 1 Peter 4:10, the word is used only by the apostle Paul. We do well to note the connection between our word *charisma* and its root word *charis*. The latter means "grace" and sets the proper basis for understanding how God gives these gifts to His people.

What Are Spiritual Gifts?

The definition offered by the respected Greek lexicographer Thayer is as good as any: "extraordinary powers, distinguishing certain Christians and enabling them to serve the church of Christ, the reception of which is due to the power of divine grace operating in their souls by the Holy Spirit."[1] My only hesitation in this description is the phrase "distinguishing certain Christians." If Thayer means "distinguishing one from another," I agree. If, however, he is implying that only certain Christians have spiritual gifts, such a view would seem to be incompatible with New Testament teaching.

Paul clearly states that spiritual gifts are given to every Christian, in the sovereignty of the Holy Spirit.

1 Corinthians 12:7 (NASB): "*To each one is given.*"

1 Corinthians 12:11 (NASB): "distributing to *each one* individually just as He wills."

Romans 12:6 (NASB): *"We have gifts that differ according to the grace given to us."*

It would seem that every Christian has at least one spiritual gift, and some have several. Perhaps multiple-gifted persons are placed by the Lord of the Church into positions of leadership as pastors, evangelists, teachers, etc.

The gift is probably not a ready-made ability to perform, but rather a capacity for service that must be developed. For example, a Christian with the gift of teaching should apply himself to training, reading, and practice to enable the Holy Spirit to produce competence in the exercise of his gift.

Ryrie is right when he reminds us that we must not be too broad in applying the concept of gift. He says a spiritual gift "is not primarily a place of service . . . a particular age group ministry."[2] No one has the gift of India or the gift of youth work or the gift of radio. What he *does* have, perhaps, is the gift of teaching and the call of God to use it with young people. Or the gift of evangelism and the call of God to India.

WHAT IS THE PURPOSE OF SPIRITUAL GIFTS?

On this question almost all evangelical scholars agree: spiritual gifts are given for the edification and spiritual growth of the Church. Edwards states it well: "Edification is the practical test by which to decide on the admission of any manifestation of power into the church and estimate the comparative value of the gifts."[3]

The relationship of chapters 12, 13, and 14 of 1 Corinthians is not accidental. The theme of this entire section is the Body of Christ and its function in unity and love. *The possession and use of spiritual gifts are inseparably bound up with the functioning Church.* One does not have the gift of evangelism to wander at will proclaiming the Gospel but to relate that gift to the Church—universal *and local.* The Body is ministered to by Christ and in turn ministers to the world.

Each smaller unit in the diagram below is part of and dependent upon the next and the whole.

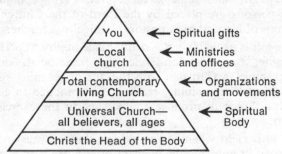

The corporate use of the gifts is basic. They are not given to "turn on" an individual but to build up the total Body. Of course, believers do not use their gifts only in the church building (not to be confused with the Church), but there must be a clear connection between the exercise of the gifts and the ongoing ministry of the total Body. Edification is the purpose, unity is the context, and love is the controlling principle or attitude for the proper exercise of spiritual gifts.

WHAT ARE THE SPIRITUAL GIFTS?

This difficult question gives rise to two related questions: How many spiritual gifts are there? And can they be categorized in any way? To both of these questions there are almost as many answers as commentators. The traditional view lists nine gifts but limits itself only to the list in 1 Corinthians 12:8-10. Most classical commentaries, like Beet, group these nine gifts into three categories such as gifts of intellectual power, miraculous power, and tongues.[4] Edwards opts for five: intellectual power, miraculous power, teaching power, critical power, and ecstatic power.[5]

More modern scholars tend toward a higher number of gifts by taking into consideration all of the passages. Theodore Epp lists eleven;[6] Ryrie, fourteen;[7] Walvoord, fifteen;[8] and Stedman, "16 or 17 basic gifts, and these may be found in various combinations within a single individual, each cluster of gifts opening the door to a wide and varied ministry."[9]

As to categories, one reads about "permanent and temporary gifts"; "motivational, ministering and manifestation gifts"; "inspired utterance, power and revelational gifts"; and "ordinary and extraordinary gifts"—to name just a few!

In this series we will look at eighteen gifts with an optional suggestion for one or two more. To avoid the arguments of category and importance, I have arranged the list in alphabetical order according to selected English words. Obviously a total of eighteen must recognize the "offices" of Ephesians 4:11 as gifts first given to men by the Spirit, and then men given to the Church by Christ. The list is intended to be exhaustive, and I believe that it includes all of the gifts available to and needed by the Church today.

Administration	Knowledge
Apostleship	Mercy
Discernment	Miracles
Evangelism	Ministering
Exhortation	Pastoring
Faith	Prophecy
Giving	Teaching
Healings	Tongues
Interpretation	Wisdom

What Is the Difference Between a Spiritual Gift and a Natural Talent?

Theologically we can say that spiritual gifts work in the spiritual realm and natural talents in the natural realm. Since all Christians are human beings, they have natural talents as well as spiritual gifts. But since not all human beings are Christians, those who do not have the Holy Spirit cannot have spiritual gifts. Even a Christian might have a natural talent for public speaking but not necessarily have the gift of prophecy.

Natural abilities (talents) benefit the whole creation through common grace. Spiritual gifts, however, are largely limited to the Church, although the presence and life of the Church in the world are a benefit to mankind generally.

Practically, we must be careful to exercise spiritual gifts in spiritual power, for natural ability cannot be the generating source for spiritual ministry. Stedman issues a valuable warning:

> The lesson is clear. Don't try to use your natural talents to accomplish the work of God, for talents cannot operate in that sphere. But use them as channels or vehicles for spiritual gifts and you will find that they dovetail beautifully. You might expect that they would do this since they both come from the same God.[10]

How Can I Tell What My Spiritual Gift Is?

Or perhaps we should talk about the plural: "gifts are." Here are four brief but realistic guidelines for recognizing how the Holy Spirit has equipped you for service:

1. What do you enjoy doing? God *does* want us to be "happy in the service of the King." Christian ministry dare not become a neurotic compulsion to duty.

2. What has God been blessing? Do you see fruit from your teaching? Are people trusting Christ as a result of your evangelism?

3. How have others encouraged you? God gives us parents, pastors, teachers, and friends to help us in making key decisions like this.

4. What has the Holy Spirit told you? The inner witness of the Spirit is not limited to confirming our salvation. He *wants* us to know what our gifts are and how we are to use them.

Other questions are worthy of our attention, but space forces limitation. For example, many ask, "When are spiritual gifts given?" Walvoord suggests, "Spiritual gifts are bestowed at that time (spiritual baptism of the believer into the body) . . . even if these gifts are not immediately observable."[11] Your gifts may be latent, waiting for activation. There may be reason to conclude that the Holy Spirit may choose at times to give a gift later in one's ministry, or even for a brief period of time (1 Ti 4:14).

Can a Christian have any gift he wants? Not really. The sovereignty of the Spirit is decisive, because He knows the needs of the Church. But we do have an interesting verse which invites us to eagerly desire the greater gifts (1 Co 12:31). One thing is clear: *No gift is the sign of superior spirituality or a higher level of walk with God. The key is not so much to seek new gifts as to recognize, develop, and use the one(s) we have.*

There are two final questions to which I cannot provide the answers. What is your spiritual gift? And what are you doing about it? Perhaps the following chapters will help you in coming to some biblical and practical conclusions.

1

THE GIFT OF ADMINISTRATION

UNCLE BILL had planned a night out, and the baby-sitter was to arrive just a few minutes after he left, to take care of Jody and Buffy until the next morning. This episode from "Family Affair," however, followed typical television situation comedy patterns when the sitter failed to show, setting the stage for an evening of high jinks by the two small children.

After a hilarious dinner of just what you might expect, Jody took over to tuck in his "little sister" for the night. As he turned out the light and prepared to leave the room, Buffy asked, "But who will tuck *you* in?" Jody rose up in his newfound chauvinism and replied, "Nobody needs to. I'm in charge, remember?" To which Buffy sighed and said, "I guess that's the trouble with people in charge. They have nobody to tuck them in."

The gift of administration is about people who don't have anybody to tuck them in. The Greek word is *kuberneseis*, meaning "helmsman" or "governor." All of its uses in Scripture refer to leadership and administration in some form of secular enterprise except where Paul impregnates the word with spiritual meaning in the Church context of 1 Corinthians 12:28.* It is a clear carry-over of the idea of organizational and superintending leader-

---

*Other uses appear in Pr 1:5; 11:14; 24:6 of the Septuagint and Ac 27:11 and Rev 18:17 in the New Testament.

15

ship. The administrator is the man who is qualified to direct the ship. Kittel puts it well when he refers to the Christian who is "a helmsman to his congregation, i.e., a true director of its order and therewith of its life."[1]

How closely this gift is to be associated with pastoral ministry is difficult to establish. Most Baptist theologians link our present form of pastoral leadership to the New Testament offices of *episkopos* and *presbuteros*, frequently translated "bishop" in many English texts. Indeed, Robertson and Plummer suggest that the *kuberneseis* "may be equivalent to *episkopoi* and *presbuteroi*."[2]

But I am not so sure. In the first place, we are dealing here primarily with a gift, not an office which might arise out of a gift. Second, while it would certainly be advantageous for all pastors to have the gift of administration, there seems to be no solid biblical teaching indicating that this gift is essential for pastoral ministry. The point is that administration must be a part of orderly Church life, and if the pastor is not gifted and trained in this aspect of spiritual ministry, who takes care of it?

The answer surely rests in the fact that most spiritual gifts are not limited to the officers of our churches. Every Christian has a spiritual gift, and a deacon, trustee, or Sunday school superintendent might very well be gifted by the Spirit for administrative ministry. It is probably not saying too much to suggest that we might well look for evidence of this gift when electing men to these and similar offices.

The idea that a layman could have the gift of administration finds scriptural basis as early as Exodus 18, where we read about Jethro, the first management consultant. His proposal for reorganization of "the church in the wilderness" was a revelation to Pastor Moses. The revision placed emphasis on such time-honored administrative principles as span of control, definition of roles, decentralization, and delegation—to say nothing of the leadership development achieved by involving scores of other men in the administrative process.

You may recall my hinting in the Introduction at two other possible gifts in addition to the eighteen already listed. One of those two must be studied in connection with the gift of *kuberneseis*. It is the word *prohistemi* in Romans 12:8 ("he that ruleth [leads], with diligence"). Barnes indicates, "This word properly designates one who is *set over* others, or who presides or rules."[3] The question is simple: Is the gift of administration the same thing as the gift of leadership? Surely Paul could have used the same word in both passages. Is there some reason why the Holy Spirit chose to distinguish these gifts?

The word *prohistemi* appears eight times in Paul's writings, usually with an emphasis upon personal leading of and care for others. A key reference is 1 Timothy 3:4, where managing or ruling one's own house and family is identified as a prerequisite for pastoral ministry (cf. 1 Ti 3:12; 5:8, 17). Some say that the context requires us to interpret leadership as linked with the gifts of "giving" and "showing mercy," which may be, they say, a reference to the administration of charitable programs (Cranfield, Lagrange, Huby, Leenhardt).

It seems to me that, in a book on spiritual gifts, one only engages in dogmatism and closure to his own peril. I prefer to think of these gifts as closely related, possibly united in a cluster for some church leaders, but not necessarily dependent one upon the other. Edwards points out one thing we do well to keep in mind these days when he reminds us, "The government of the Corinthian church at this time was a pure democracy [in which] . . . the function of teaching was often separated from that of ruling."[4] And, I would add, the function of ruling was often separated from that of pastoring. The "strong man" monolithic churches of our day seem to have frail basis in a proper understanding of New Testament gifts, even the necessary and *spiritual* gift of administration.

2

THE GIFT OF APOSTLESHIP

Is THERE A DIFFERENCE between the disciples and the apostles? Most evangelical scholars believe there is, and for good textual reasons. The Great Commission commands a "discipling" of all nations, and one gets the clear impression that all believers are called to a life of discipleship. The "twelve apostles" are frequently called disciples in the gospels, but the term "apostle" is broadened in the early church.

The noun *apostole* appears four times in the New Testament with no dramatic insight into the role of the gift (Ac 1:25; Ro 1:5; 1 Co 9:2; Gal 2:8). One reason for including apostleship in this book is the unique position of the idea in 1 Corinthians 12:28 and Ephesians 4:11. In both passages, of course, it is primarily viewed as an office, and perhaps that is Paul's only point of emphasis. But the intertwining relationship between gifts and offices in the New Testament leads me to explore the possibility of a *gift* of apostleship as well.

Originally the word *apostle* meant one who was commissioned as the commander of a fleet of ships. This interesting parallel with the gift of administration helps us to see the leadership stature inherent in the proper use of spiritual gifts. One chosen as an apostle would possess great authority, stand under direct orders from the chief

18

of staff, and be required to do extensive traveling, often in foreign lands.

The New Testament use of the word does not depart widely from its basic root meaning. An apostle was one commissioned by the Lord, sent into the world under orders, with a specific message from his Superior. *Messenger* conveys part of the concept, but fails to relate the authoritative nature of the apostolic gift.

During the days of the early Church the apostles equipped the saints by drawing them into working units, teaching them God's truth, and ordaining leaders for the local groups. Their lives were examples of holy living (see 1 Th 1), and their messages considered orders from headquarters for the young churches.

The apostle Paul certainly demonstrates the priority of this office in God's order of church life. Combining various apparent gifts with several offices, he is a walking symbol of the blend of these two elements of spiritual dynamic. Godet says, "The apostolate continues the two sides of gift and office, both raised to their highest power."[1]

Ephesians 4:11 also treats this unique union. Here men who *have* spiritual gifts become *themselves* spiritual gifts to the Church. I assume that the five gift offices mentioned in this verse can be considered gifts first, then offices.

Of course the crucial question has to do with the possibility of one possessing the gift of apostleship in our day. Lange is willing to stretch the term beyond the first century to apply to "those men, chosen specially endowed by the Lord, appointed to found churches, as Boniface the Apostle of the Germans, Egede the Apostle of Greenland, Ziegenbalg and Schwartz the Apostles of India."[2]

Boniface lived in the eighth century and Ziegenbalg was taking a furlough as late as 1715! So why not think of Carey and Judson as apostles and, with a bit of flexibility, church-planting missionaries on almost every continent today?

Is it possible for us to conceive of a separation of **gift**

and office after the first century? Rather than assigning
this gift to the history of the early Church, can we not
recognize the broad sense of the verb form *apostello* ("to
send on a mission")? Could it not be that all through
the years the Holy Spirit has given this gift to God's people
in what we have come to call "missionary service"?

Many have chosen the option of locking several of the
spiritual gifts into the first century lest some explanation
be required for their presence in the Church today. I
would prefer to allow the Holy Spirit the broadest latitude
to produce in Christ's Body any gift in any age as He sees
fit. It seems to be quite safe to say that the *office* of the
apostles was restricted to the establishing of the New
Testament church. But if Lange is right in stretching that
term through missionary history, we may be justified in
seeing evidence of apostleship not only as a gift but a gift
which has operated in the Church throughout all the years
of its history.

3

THE GIFT OF DISCERNMENT

IN THE UNITED STATES House of Representatives there is that trophy of burcaucracy, the Committee on Committees. Presumably its purpose is to coordinate and regulate the membership, activities, and production of the multiple committee functions of the parent body.

In a similar way, the gift of discernment might be called a "gift on gifts." A. T. Robertson says that it is given "to tell whether the gifts were really of the Holy Spirit and supernatural . . . or merely strange though natural, or even diabolical."[1] Indeed, if there were no gift of discernment available in the theological miasma of the late twentieth century, God would have to invent one to help us find our way in the fog.

The noun form used in 1 Corinthians 12:10 (NASB): ("distinguishing of spirits") is *diakrisis*—from *diakrino*, meaning to judge or evaluate. This gift seems to be closely linked with that of prophecy both here and in 14:29, although surely a wider reference can be seen to all gifts of public ministry. Elsewhere in the New Testament the early Church leaders call for discernment on the part of God's people without always naming it as a gift (1 Th 5:21; 1 Jn 4:1).

More is involved in the gift of discernment than the serious scriptural comparison for which Luke commended the Bereans, as noble and necessary as that is (Ac 17:10-

11). As a divinely given spiritual gift, this depth-level discernment allows the user to intuitively identify truth from error because he has been provided with supernatural analysis. Tongues must be interpreted; prophecy must be discerned. Today, as in the first century, false prophets abound, even within the broad fences of Christendom. Every believer is to test the written and spoken words of religious leaders by their allegiance to God's inscripturated Word. But to some there is apparently given a special "power of discerning between the true and the false spirit . . . a faculty to apply the test."[2]

The frightening phenomenon of fascination with witchcraft and the occult in our day calls forth new attention to the gift of discernment. Once the weird ware of storefront churches in San Francisco, the occult has now "gone respectable." Endor is emerging on college and university campuses from coast to coast, filling classrooms with entranced followers or curious skeptics. *Newsweek* reports, "Courses in a wide variety of occult subjects are now among the most popular additions to the curriculum at many schools."[3]

Of course the gift of discernment is probably not limited to an analysis of demonism. Perhaps we could identify three types of uses in the Church.

1. That which we have just described, an evaluation of the spirits to determine which are of God and which of Satan, particularly with respect to prophecy.

2. An awareness, most likely through inner witness of the Spirit in heart and mind, of the intrusion of human elements into worship. I use the term *human* here in the sense of "carnal" or "fleshly." It is quite possible that the truly Christ-oriented character our services should portray can be stained by the one who seeks to glorify himself and not the Lord of grace.

3. Discernment of the Spirit's presence and working in other people. This could take form in nonverbal communication between two believers who have not previous-

ly met, but who, upon meeting, sense the Holy Spirit's dwelling in each other. Another feature of this level of the gift might be the differentiation between demon influence and mental illness. Many Christian psychologists believe both are possible, and God could use this gift to allow understanding of the cause of abnormal behavior.

How can one tell if he has the gift of discernment? The reader is referred back to the Introduction for some general guidelines. But with respect to this particular gift we do well to keep in mind the various levels or functions the ministry of discernment seems to take in the New Testament. Let me call them "natural," "spiritual," and "gifted."

Natural discernment is possible for every man, Christian or not. Sometimes we call it "good judgment" or "horse sense." It is the ability to make wise decisions by observing and understanding inputs and potential outcomes. Some people seem to have more of this than others, but it is also a skill which can be learned.

Spiritual discernment comes to a believer as he grows in Christ (Ep 4:14-15). It is inseparably connected with knowledge of the Bible and the process of spiritual maturing carried out in our lives by the Holy Spirit.

By *gifted discernment* I mean to suggest that the Holy Spirit gives to some believers a special gift, enabling them to serve the Church as watchmen, able to identify spiritual untruth by supernatural insight. Like many of the other gifts, this one could lead to pride and perverted use in character assassination and harsh criticism. But it will not if we remember that all gifts are of grace and for the benefit of the Church and must be exercised in love.

4

THE GIFT OF EVANGELISM

As UNUSUAL as it may seem, the word evangelist (*euange-listes*) appears only three times in the New Testament: Acts 21:8; Ephesians 4:11; 2 Timothy 4:5. The word should not be construed to mean "soul winner," because it conveys only the more specific delineation of communicating the Gospel, that is, "one who shares the good news." William Barclay refers to evangelists as "the rank and file missionaries of the church."[1]

Of these three texts, Ephesians 4:11 is the only one which puts evangelism on the list of the spiritual gifts. It is possible, of course, that the items in this verse are a reference only to offices and not to gifts. I have taken the position, however, that the relationship of these ministries to previously mentioned charisms is sufficient evidence to suggest that the persons of verse 11 have been first gifted in accordance with the pattern of 1 Corinthians 12, and then, in turn, given as gifts to the Church.

The itinerating nature of the first-century evangelists is exemplified by Philip in the Acts 21 passage. The evangelist proclaimed the redemptive message of the Gospel and then moved on to proclaim it elsewhere. Meanwhile the pastors and teachers set about the task of edifying the congregation.

At different times it would appear that the same individual applied both of these offices. Paul, for example,

24

planted churches on the first missionary journey (evangelism) which he nurtured and built up in the faith on the second trip (teaching). And Timothy was probably a pastor-teacher at Ephesus, yet Paul writes the reminder, "Do the work of an evangelist."

Two peripheral yet important ideas connected with spiritual gifts bear mentioning here. First of all, we should ask whether it is possible to have a spiritual gift "for a time," that is, on a temporary basis. Apparently evangelism was not Timothy's primary gift, but he was to engage in it as a part of his other duties.

I have never forgotten a story which I heard Dr. George Peters of Dallas Theological Seminary tell about his own ministry. It is related here from memory, so all of the details may not be completely accurate. Apparently a mission representative from some South American country called to ask Dr. Peters if he could spend some time during the summer ministering on the field. Dr. Peters responded affirmatively until he understood that the task would be the conducting of evangelistic campaigns. Then the conversation sounded something like this:

"I'm sorry, but I'm afraid I shouldn't come. You see, I have the gift of teaching, not the gift of evangelism."

"But, Dr. Peters, if we pray that God will give you the gift of evangelism for this ministry here, and if you believe He has answered our prayer, then will you accept our invitation?"

"Yes, if you put it that way, let's see how the Holy Spirit responds."

Dr. Peters testifies that he received the gift of evangelism for that month of ministry only and then returned to the use of the gift of teaching in the fall.

No one likes to build a theology of experience less than I, but there does seem to be evidence that the Holy Spirit's sovereign control over spiritual gifts may allow room for thinking about "temporary" gifts for specific, short-term service.

The other point of caution I wish to offer here is a reminder that one does not have to have the full gift of a ministry in order to be held responsible for following God's commands to serve. For example, perhaps not every Sunday school teacher has the *gift* of teaching, but the Spirit may still enable such persons to carry out an effective ministry. Actually, every Christian parent is required to be a teacher, but surely not all parents have the gift of teaching.

Walvoord points out the same thing about evangelism: "While all are called to bring the gospel to the lost by whatever means may be at their disposal, . . . it is the sovereign purpose of God that certain men should have a special gift in evangelism."[2] To put it very simply, one does not have to be Billy Graham in order to share his faith with others.

MacPherson suggests that the term *evangelist* (like *apostle* and *prophet*) designated a high office in the first-century Church, and "though the offices were not continued, many of the most characteristic of the gifts which qualified for these offices are found to be in the possession of individual holders of the permanent ministerial office."[3] This may be a significant clue to our understanding of how spiritual gifts operate today. Before the completed canon, it was essential for the Church to have authoritative revelatory voices from God, so that the possession of many of the gifts was tantamount to holding office. But now the gifts reflect to the Word (God *has* spoken—in writing), and the gifts help us to understand what He has said and then to explain it to others.

With the possible exception of Timothy's unique ministry (probably oversight over several congregations), almost all references to evangelism and evangelists focus on the "scattered church." In their collective gatherings the early Church emphasized worship, nurture, and fellowship—one does not evangelize believers. Yet we have inverted the formula a bit, often thinking that the church building is the fitting place for people to "get saved." It seems that we are seeing in this decade, however, a return to one-to-one witnessing and informal faith-sharing which characterized the early Church's understanding of evangelism.

5

THE GIFT OF EXHORTATION

WHEN JESUS taught the disciples how to react to His death, resurrection, and ascension, one of the crucial problems was the impending vacuum of His absence. "Lord, to whom shall we go?" was the childlike quality of their faith throughout their three and one half years of experience with the incarnate Lord.

Seeking to alleviate their fear of the unknown, as well as teach them some basic New Testament pneumatology, the Master explained that the Father would be sending "another Helper" (Jn 14:16, NASB). We have come to know the Greek term used to describe the Holy Spirit in this passage as the word *paraclete* (one who is called alongside to comfort and counsel).

Two similar forms of this word appear in Romans 12:8 to introduce the charism (gift) of exhortation. Throughout Scripture the concept of exhortation has a double meaning: to comfort or encourage, and to admonish. Rather than stressing one to the minimizing of the other, we might profit by remembering the family orientation of the Bible. A good father is regularly engaged in both aspects of exhortation, sometimes in connection with the same incident within a few minutes of time. Paul even uses the paternal image as an example of exhortation in the leadership role of the Church (1 Th 2:11).

In the arena of congregational life, there is a constant

28

need for most pastors to exercise the gift of *paraklesis* (exhortation). Paul frequently called the believers together for exhortation, which was usually a combination of challenge and comfort (Ac 11:23; 14:22; 15:32). The gift is closely (but not inseparably) connected with the gift of prophecy (1 Co 14:31; 1 Ti 4:13-14), another suggestion that it is often exercised within the pastoral office.

In studying the original text of Romans 12, one is impressed by the fact that the same word appears in verse 1 translated in the King James Version by the English word "beseech," and in the New American Standard Bible, "urge." The strong sense of urgency certainly implies that the Christian's use of the gift of exhortation is not only passive and nondirective encouragement, but also quite explicit advice.

Which leads me to mention the current controversy in Christian counseling over the role and procedures of the counselor. In secular psychology the revolt against the purely nondirective pattern has been led by reality therapists like Glasser and Mowrer. Evangelicals have been introduced to this individual responsibility theme through Jay Adams' *Competent to Counsel*. (The same basic thrust is discernible in the writings of Trobisch.) Adams talks about "nouthetic counseling" and "confrontation," emphasizing the role of God's absolute truth in dealing with the counselee's problems.

One does not need to opt for exclusively directive or nondirective counseling to recognize that the gift of *paraklesis* relates to both. Counseling is a process, not a gift, so it would be improper to equate the two and identify *paraklesis* as "the gift of counseling." The gift has a broader application in preaching, teaching, and informal conversations between and among believers. It may very well be, however, that just as certain people gifted in *euangelistes* become "evangelists," so persons gifted in *paraklesis* become "counselors."

Exhortation is therefore both a public and a private ministry. It is limited neither to pulpit nor pew, to leader nor layman. I know a young Christian mother who has been through serious physical suffering. Now it is humanly inexplicable how the Holy Spirit causes her to cross paths with others just as they learn of some tragedy in their own lives. She may very well have the gift of exhortation.

Perhaps another common use of the gift is through song. There is no "gift of music" in the strict sense of charisma. Music is a general grace to all mankind. But "singing and making melody" (Eph 5:19), when the theology is sound and the musician Spirit-filled, is surely a superb way of exhorting the Church in public ministry. Choir members, neglect not the gift that may be in you!

Because of the close connection between "teaching" and "exhortation" in Romans 12 and their common ultimate purpose (edification), some have thought to tie them together more closely than the text seems to imply. Teaching focuses on the communication of content, whereas exhortation is, to borrow Cranfield's phrase, "to help Christians to live out their obedience to the gospel."[1] Luther once noted, "Teaching and exhortation differ from each other in this, that teaching is directed to the ignorant but exhortation to those who have knowledge."[2] And Barnes helpfully adds, "This word [*paraklesis*] properly denotes one who urges to the *practical* duties of religion, in distinction from one who teaches its doctrines. One who presents the *warnings* and *promises* of God to excite men to the discharge of their duty."[3]

These are days of "people emphasis" in our churches. We are turning away from a focus on programs to a more biblical focus on persons. It is a good day, then, to reconsider, restore, and refresh the gift of exhortation among our congregations, not only in sermon and private office, but also in the sharing of the body from house to house, seeking to mutually edify itself in love.

6

THE GIFT OF FAITH

SINCE BY GOD'S GRACE every Christian has exercised faith in Christ's finished work in order to enter into his status as a justified member of the family of God, some find it difficult to see how faith can be a special gift—an endowment for ministry in the Church. Although the word is the same (*pistis*), the context of 1 Corinthians 12:9; 13:2; and Romans 12:6 demands an interpretation consistent with our understanding of the nature of spiritual gifts. The gift of faith is also not to be equated with the fruit of faith described in Galatians 5:22. A. T. Robertson well says of 1 Corinthians 12:9, "Not faith of surrender, saving faith, but wonder-working faith."[1]

The term "wonder-working" may be just a bit misleading. This faith does not *produce* the work of God but rather *sets the climate* or atmosphere in which God chooses to unleash His miracle-working power. Such faith is neither blind nor irrational. It does not drift aimlessly in search of a destination. Rather, like a piece of steel to its compelling magnet, it attaches itself to the Sovereign of the universe.

The person who demonstrates the gift of faith is characterized by his utter dependence upon the Lord. He puts little stock in human resources; and even when they are available, he realizes that God has indirectly supplied them through the human donor.

The Bible abounds with examples of this kind of faith. Their tribute is written in Hebrews 11, which, in its selective format, makes no attempt to be exhaustive. Consider:

Abel and his sacrifice

Noah and his unorthodox carpentry

Abraham staring down at Isaac on the altar

Moses and his vision of freedom

Joshua and his commitment to victory

David and his assurance that God would give him the kingdom in His good time

And such faith was no stranger in the days of the New Testament.

John the Baptist daily scanned the burning sands for the promised Messiah.

Twelve men gave up their jobs and homes to follow an itinerant Teacher.

Barnabas gave everything he had to the fledgling Church.

Paul and Silas sang praises at midnight in a Philippian jail.

Thousands of early Christians looked to God to sustain them in the midst of pagan surroundings.

John wrote his visions of an eternal city which would someday house all those who love the Lamb.

What does such a spiritual gift mean to the Church today? Precisely the same dynamic for growth which it has always signified! There are building programs to be started, outreach to be secured, educational programs to be sustained, missionaries to be sent, colleges and seminaries to be supported, and saints to be stirred.

And to some of our leaders the Holy Spirit gives the gift of faith. These gifted men and women become the dreamers and visionaries among us. They see beyond the current crop of problems and are not stymied by the "seven last words of the church" ("We've never done it that way before"). Sometimes their assurance that God *will* come through for His people is frustrating to others who want to be more "practical" and "realistic." But Christ, the Lord of the Church, knows that our progress is dependent upon faith leadership.

The gift of faith is not necessarily to be equated with deficit budgeting. Mortgage programs are not wrong, and indeed are often necessary. But sometimes we overextend God's credit without asking Him about it, then call it faith when, in desperation, we call on Him to redeem His good reputation.

A primary characteristic of all spiritual gifts, and therefore of faith, is their supernatural origin. We should not confuse our general ability to believe God's Word (probably a result of the *fruit* of faith) with a unique assurance that something which we believe to be in God's plan will definitely come to pass. There is an important difference here between an *assenting* and *appropriating* faith.

Appropriating faith is never the result of human ability or strength. It cannot be generated by our own wills, no matter how desperately we attempt to conjure it up. Spiritual gifts are given sovereignly. Certainly it is proper and biblical to pray for the gift of faith, but not to demand that God succumb to our analysis of what gifts we need and could best use. This lesson was learned by the embarrassed disciples when their best healing efforts counted for nothing on an epileptic boy (Mt 17:14-21).

In this last third of the twentieth century we live in an era of unprecedented self-dependence. Man and his machines bow together at the shrine of science, confident that nothing is ultimately impossible. The spirit of the age revolts against a supernaturalism which looks to heaven expecting divine intervention in behalf of the people of God.

But perhaps, after years of human effort, the Church is ready in this decade to become again the unique possession of a unique God. Perhaps men and women with the gift of faith can lead us in "looking to Jesus" as did the faith heroes of Hebrews 11. Perhaps amid all our affluence and materialism, the vitality of Judson and Mueller can live again.

7

THE GIFT OF GIVING

It is perhaps appropriate that our study of the gift of
giving in this book should follow our study of the gift of
faith, for they are connected at the point of material
support for the work of the Church.

That is not to say that either gift concerns itself only,
or even primarily, with money. Indeed, Lenski takes the
key passage (Ro 12:8) to be a "reference to spiritual
impartation" as the word is used in Romans 1:11 and
1 Thessalonians 2:8.[1] No doubt the issue of giving of
one's own spiritual resources is a significant part of the
mutually edifying body. But there seems to be ample evidence for taking the reference here to be a directive
toward distributing one's wealth to others in the name of
Christ and for the sake of His Church.

To put it most simply then, the one who has the gift
of giving donates generously to others out of his own
resources and does it cheerfully because it is a gift and
not a duty. We would tend, I think, to refer such a gift
to the few wealthy among us. But God's work has always
been primarily supported by those of modest means.

To be sure, we welcome the gifts of the wealthy and
are delighted if a millionaire recognizes the gift of giving
in response to a fund drive at the denominational college.
But let us honestly recognize that, in the sovereignty

of the Holy Spirit, the middle- or lower-income Christian can also receive the gift of giving.

It is important to remember that the basic context for the utilization of spiritual gifts is the local church. Sometimes believers give to every cause, social and religious, while allowing the home congregation to stagger along under the burden of inadequate finances. Griffith Thomas puts it well when he reminds us that the giver "is to do it with liberality, communicating freely of his own possessions for the good of the community."[2]

Perhaps we can say that there are two characteristics of the person who has the gift of giving: He has resources from which he may give, and he delights in sharing those resources with others. We like to focus upon the more glamorous or controversial gifts, but where would our pastors and teachers be without the support of those who properly employ the gift of giving?

And if it is possible to request a gift from God (as I have previously suggested), then those who ask God to prosper their business ventures and investments in order that they may give more to the Lord's work are opting for a biblical pattern. But attitude is as important as ability in exercising any spiritual gift, and this one is certainly no exception. The man who writes a check for half a million dollars to Alpha and Omega Christian College in order to get his name on a plaque, a seat on the board, or prestige in the church is not exercising the spiritual gift of giving (of course that does not mean Alpha and Omega will turn down the money).

The word *haplotes*, translated "simplicity" in the King James Version, is of crucial importance here. The word is variously translated as "liberality," "cheerfulness," etc., but the underlying meaning is "joyful eagerness." How many Christians give to God's work with a "joyful eagerness"? Such an attitude is obviously significantly different from "devoted duty" or even "loyalty to the church."

Godet offers a helpful discussion of the word *haplotes*.

> According to its etymological meaning, the word
> signifies: the disposition not to turn back on oneself; and
> it is obvious that from this first meaning there may fol-
> low either that of *generosity*, when man gives without
> letting himself be arrested by any selfish calculation, or
> that of *simplicity*, when he gives without his left hand
> knowing what his right does—that is to say without any
> vain going back on himself, and without any air of
> haughtiness.[3]

With the exception of one use by James (1:5), *haplotes*
is a distinctive Pauline term employed by the apostle
seven times in addition to our text in Romans 12:8. Five
out of the seven references are in the book of 2 Corinthians, and three of them clearly refer to money.

This spiritual attitude toward giving reminds us of the
teaching of Christ in Matthew 6:1-4. The "left hand-
right hand" injunction is descriptive of an attitude of humility and grace rather than pride and legalism in one's
giving. Giving with pretention and public clamor is an act
of hypocrisy, not the exercise of a spiritual gift.

One more thought. If we can ask people to exercise
other spiritual gifts for the benefit of the Church, why
are we so hesitant and apologetic about asking people to
put the gift of giving into practice? Furthermore,
shouldn't we provide some way in which God's people
can develop this spiritual gift? We conduct leadership
training sessions for teachers and pastors, but some still
view stewardship and the asking for money as an evidence
of carnality.

Perhaps we still labor under the often misquoted version of a famous statement: "Money is the root of all
evil." But that is *not* what Paul said. He warned Timothy
"The *love* of money is the root of all evil" (I Ti 6:10),
thereby emphasizing again that, in giving, the attitude is
more important than the act.

So let us rally to the cross those people who have this necessary spiritual gift. Let us show them that it is not carnal but spiritual to recognize and use their gift. And while we're at it, let us engage in a bit of self-examination to see if the Spirit may have given us the gift of giving.

8

THE GIFT OF HEALING

IN ATTEMPTING to honestly treat all the spiritual gifts listed in the Bible, one runs into great difficulty with two or three, the gift of healing among them. The difficulty arises primarily because of the controversy which surrounds these gifts in the various interpretations held within the evangelical camp.

Viewpoints are often marked by extremes. Consider the following popular approaches to the gift of healing:

1. Anyone with the gift of healing has the ability to heal at will.

2. Healing is entirely dependent upon the faith of the sick person.

3. The gift of healing was only for New Testament times—it does not exist at all today.

Part of our problem doubtless stems from the abuse and perversion of many self-styled "healers" in our day. But there are surely just as many charlatan "evangelists" (e.g., Marjoe and company), yet few question the reality of the gift of evangelism. Emotions run high for and against almost every interpretation of healing, but let us take another look at the Scriptures.

The word for "healing" is *iama*, which appears in 1 Corinthians 12:9, 28, 30. These are the only New Testament uses of the word, though it is common in the Septuagint (Greek version of the Old Testament). Kittel describes it well within its biblical context:

The gift of healing is an operation of the name of the exalted Christ. To put the same thing in another way, it is an operation of the ascended Lord through the Spirit (Acts 9:34; Rom. 15:18 f.). It does not belong to the essence of the Christian state. It is an individual gift of grace.[1]

From Kittel's definition and, more important, from New Testament patterns, it is clear that only Christ has authority to heal, and only He can direct how that authority should be used. To properly understand this central fact frees the Church from demanding that everyone be healed, or making "lack of faith" the cause for failure.

It is worth our attention to note that the plural is used for both words each time the expression appears: that is, "gifts of healing." Hillis suggests that there is an implication therefore that "each separate healing is a separate gift."[2] Stedman, on the other hand, refers the plural to "healing at every level of human need: bodily, emotionally and spiritually."[3] Perhaps this latter suggestion is closer to the thrust of the text, though reputable commentators support both conclusions.

The crucial, practical question, of course, is: Are the "gifts of healings" available today? Like Tevye I can confidently proclaim, "I don't know." It seems to me that blatant dogmatism either affirming or denying the contemporaneity of any of the gifts is a tenuous position. On a recent trip to Southeast Asia I talked with Indonesian students at the Singapore Bible College who claimed to have seen many incidents of physical healing during that country's revivals.

Others, like theologians Walvoord and Ryrie, take the position that healing "ceased as a gift with the passing of the apostles."[4] To my knowledge, no genuine Evangelical doubts God's ability to heal. The question centers on healing as a spiritual *gift* for the Church in our day.

Some writers choose a cautious middle ground, and I

prefer to cast my lot with them. Stedman, for example, claims that physical healing "is a rare gift today, infrequently bestowed." In responding to the question, Why? he suggests, "It is not the will of the Spirit for it to be given in these days as widely as it was in the early church."[5] Stedman does see ample evidence of the gift of healing at the mental and emotional levels of disease.

A similar view is expressed by international Bible teacher Alan Redpath:

> Healing is a gift, and I believe without any shadow of doubt God has given it to some—the ability to command disease to be removed from a human body in the name of the Lord. But I believe that for every ten who practice the gift, probably only one has it in the sovereignty of God. There is no gift so trafficked with and commercialized today as this one.[6]

This fear of the fraudulent is a rational one widely shared among Christians. The Marjoe strain has haunted the American church for many years. But phony replicas are usually predicated upon reality, and we must be careful not to condemn by unwarranted sweeping generalizations. It is neither good logic nor good theology to say, "I never met a person who has the gift of healing; therefore, the gift is not given today."

In July 1973, *Christianity Today* published an exclusive interview with Kathryn Kuhlman, whom the editors call "the best-known woman preacher in the world." Any objective reader will be forced to conclude that her responses to penetrating questions represent a pleasant contrast to some of the ego-oriented "healers" we have seen in our generation.

When asked, "Do you feel you have the gift of healing?" Miss Kuhlman expresses modesty in her reply by saying:

I would never say that I have ever received any gift. I am leery of folks who boast of this or that gift. The greatest of the Christian graces is humility. All that I know is that I have yielded my body to Him to be filled with the Holy Spirit ... when the Holy Spirit is lifted from me I am the most ordinary person that ever lived.[7]

Does Kathryn Kuhlman have the gift of healing? Does anyone else in the world today? My previous answer persists: I don't know. But the caution Miss Kuhlman displayed in the *Christianity Today* interview is the kind of moderation becoming to all thinking believers with respect to conclusions about the gifts of healing.

9

THE GIFT OF INTERPRETATION

IT IS AN AXIOM of planning and decision making that one's immediate choices place restrictions upon future choices. I find myself caught in that web now. Having determined to treat the spiritual gifts alphabetically to avoid any hint of category or preference, it becomes necessary to deal with the gift of interpretation before treating the gift of tongues. Yet the inseparability of the two is obvious, even to the most casual Bible student.

So this becomes, in effect, a contingency section in the book, dependent upon the conclusions reached in the analysis of the gift of tongues. Perhaps it is best then to confine the present discussion to what the gift of interpretation was in New Testament times and leave open any attempt to delineate what it may or may not be today.

The Greek word in question is *hermeneia*, translated two times in the New American Standard Bible and King James Version by the word "interpretation" (1 Co 12: 10; 14:26). The verb form, *diermeneuo*, is more common, appearing six times,* and a noun construct meaning "interpreter" is used in 1 Corinthians 14:28 (*diermeneutes*). A closely related term, *ermeneuo*, is used three times by John (1:38, 42; 9:7) and once by the writer of the book of Hebrews (7:2).

---

*Lk 24:27; Ac 9:36; 1 Co 12:30; 14:5, 13, 27.

In some references the definition of the various terms is clear: to translate from one language to another (e.g., Ac 9:36, NASB: "a certain disciple named Tabitha [which translated in Greek is called Dorcas]"). But the appearances in 1 Corinthians 12 and 14 are woven into a seamless garment with the matter of speaking in tongues and therefore deal with interpretation as a distinct gift of the Spirit.

In these chapters one must define interpretation in harmony with his understanding of tongues. If tongues were translatable languages, then interpretation had to do with giving the meaning of the speaker's words in the language common to the gathered group. On the other hand, if tongues were ecstatic utterances and no language at all, then interpretation was, as Lange puts it, "an ability which implied the power of bringing the understanding (*nous*) to bear upon the meaning of the things wrought by the Spirit, and thus to consciously apprehend them."[1]

In either case, neither the words nor their contexts required an exact word-by-word translation of the message but rather a revelation by the Holy Spirit displaying the meaning of the utterance. It is important to note that meaning and understanding are key ideas in Paul's treatment of this gift. It is not the *experience* of tongue-speaking which is in focus but rather the *communication* of God-given ideas through interpretation.

The clear purpose of the gift is the edification of the Church. That is why the word(s) appear five times in 1 Corinthians 14, which deals with the upbuilding ministry of public worship.† Apparently the gift could be given to the same individual who exercised the gift of tongues (v. 13) or to another person in the group (v. 27).

If there is no interpreter present, the tongue-speaker must confine himself to private exercise of his gift (v. 28).

---

†This chapter is treated at greater length in chap. 15 on the gift of prophecy.

The chapter surely suggests that one who knows he has the gift of tongues should determine in advance of a public meeting whether or not one with the gift of interpretation is to be present. Such careful attention to the use of spiritual gifts was essential to the order God wanted to maintain in congregational life (v. 33, 40).

Edification is nurtured in an atmosphere of design and properly disciplined behavior. Noise and pandemonium merely distort the attitudes and emotions of the worshipers and distract from necessary understanding. The orderliness of Christian worship stood in contrast to first-century paganism. As Robertson notes, "It seems clear that this ecstatic utterance was not uncontrollable; it was very different from the frenzy of some heathen rites, in which the worshiper parted with both reason and power of will."[2] And though order was achieved by limiting number and succession of speakers, the key to edification was the gift of interpretation.

If a tongue-speaker does not himself have the gift of interpretation, and if an entire congregation is dependent upon one interpreter to receive a message from God through tongues, it seems to be a situation fraught with danger. When the pastor preaches, we can check his explanations by comparing them with Scripture and commentaries. But in listening to an interpreter of a tongue, the congregation is apparently at the mercy of the interpreter.

One can see how such a gift could be misused. Smith goes so far as to say:

> In every case where a claim to have the gift of interpretation of tongues has been weighed, it has been found wanting. Scientific analysis has pointed out that there is no relationship between the tongues and the supposed interpretation.[3]

Though dogmatism dampens my enthusiasm for his case, Smith does point up a danger we do well to heed.

Since interpretation is the key to meaning, it stands in a place of even greater importance than the gift of tongues, though either one without the other is meaningless toward the goal of edification.

10

THE GIFT OF KNOWLEDGE

SOME OF THE WORDS used to identify spiritual gifts are quite rare. Terms like *kuberneisis* (administration), for example, can be tracked down in a thorough word study in order to catch nuances of meaning which serve as clues to interpretation.

Such is not the case, however, with *gnosis* (knowledge), one of the more common terms in the New Testament. There is little difficulty in arriving at a general definition of the term. The hermeneutical trick is to clarify the unique contextual usage in 1 Corinthians 12:8 (NASB): "and to another the word [utterance] of knowledge according to the same Spirit." To be specific, what is the gift of knowledge?

Any attempt at honest exegesis must recognize the relationship between knowledge and wisdom in this verse. And on this issue the commentators are not uniformly agreed. Here are some sample "explanations":

Lange—"We might take the distinction between these two to be that of theoretical and practical knowledge."[1]

Edwards—"Wisdom was the prerogative of the mature Christian, knowledge was available to immature as well."[2]

Beet—"*Knowledge* is mere acquaintance with things past, present or future. *Wisdom* is, from the Christian point of view, such a direct grasp of underlying principles and eternal realities as enables a man to choose the right goal and the best path in life."[3]

47

Godet—"We shall rather see in *gnosis* a notion of effort, investigation, discovery . . . and in *sophia* [wisdom], on the contrary, the idea of a calm possession of truth already acquired, as well as of its practical applications."[4]

Calvin—"Let us then take *knowledge* as meaning *ordinary information*, and *wisdom*, as including revelations that are of a more secret and sublime order."[5]

We examine this relationship further in chapter 18 on wisdom, but there does seem to be an emphasis upon wisdom as being both a deeper and more practical understanding of truth.

But we may ask, what kind of knowledge is in view in the spiritual gift? Robertson uses the words *insight* and *illumination* to describe the intellectual process involved.[6] The uses of the word in 1 Corinthians indicate that Paul intends to combat a pseudospiritual intellectualism in Corinth (8:1-2).

There is also a link between the New Testament concept of "mystery" and the gift of knowledge to understand those mysteries (13:2). Since the revelation of the mysteries was supernatural, the interpretation is also supernatural.

There doubtless was a time in the early days of the Church when knowledge was a revelational gift, that is, God gave new truth to indicate His plan to man. But that was before the completion of the canon of Scripture.

Now knowledge seems to be interpretive in function, leading the recipient of the gift into an understanding of God's revealed truth concerning the unfolding of His work in the world (Eph 3:3-6). Because of this deeper "enlightenment," the gift of knowledge, by its very visibility, tends to "puff up." Knowledge brings power and, therefore, the temptation to take a superior attitude toward others.

This gift is a prime example of how spiritual gifts need to be developed. Godet reminds us that "knowledge advances by means of subjective and deliberate study, which, if it is not to deviate from the straight line of divine truth, must be carried on according to the light of the Spirit."[7] Perhaps we can say that the gift of knowledge is most evident in Christian scholars who research, investigate, interpret, and explain God's special and natural revelation.

In my judgment, the ultimate key to understanding the gift of knowledge is found in 1 Corinthians 2:11-16. Here Paul identifies a level of understanding which is beyond the natural man: "But a natural man does not accept the things of the Spirit of God; for they are foolishness to him, and he cannot understand [know] them, because they are spiritually appraised" (v. 14, NASB).

In context the passage indicates that spiritual truths are also not clearly understood by carnal Christians. Only those who have spiritual mentality can really come to grips with biblical interpretation. And apparently there is a level of understanding God's truth which is reserved for those to whom the Holy Spirit has chosen to give the gift of knowledge.

Certainly we would be less than wise to miss the obvious connection between and among several spiritual gifts which have to do with study and perception: knowledge, wisdom, teaching, prophecy, and possibly administration. Perhaps we need to get a fresh insight today into the Church's need for knowledge to combat, or at least balance, the surging tide of experiential theology so popular in the 1970s.

11

THE GIFT OF MERCY

OH, THAT we would give greater emphasis to the less dramatic and spectacular spiritual gifts! The gift of showing mercy or lovingkindness (Ro 12:8) is a beautiful example of the type of personal care needed by thousands of "hurting" people in our congregations. When our theological debates about tongues and healings have left us cold and disunited, let us turn to gifts like this one in our efforts to minister to the Church—the only real purpose of any spiritual gift.

Godet defines the gift well:

> He that showeth mercy denotes the believer who feels called to devote himself to the visiting of the sick and afflicted. There is a gift of sympathy which particularly fits for this sort of work, and which is, as it were, the key to open the heart of the sufferer.[1]

Showing mercy is a "personal" rather than "official" ministry. Some gifts are inseparably related to an office in the congregation—like pastoring or apostleship—but here we seem to be focusing upon a service dependent more upon personal need than corporate organization. Of course, it is possible that those who have this gift can be recognized by the church and designated to perform their service in conjunction with the total life of the congregation.

50

Some churches are responding to the lay-leadership awareness of this decade by assigning more "pastoral" duties to their deacons. The Southern Baptist Convention's deacon-care program is perhaps the most detailed in organization. In such a program the gift of mercy is a crucial one for those serving in such "caring" ministries. One pastor describes his experience with a deacon-care program in these words:

> In the church I am now serving, each deacon is assigned a proportionate number of families within the congregation. These families are under his care for a given year. In addition to interest and concern from the pastor and the church staff, each family has a deacon who will offer special friendship as the need arises.[2]

Nothing in Scripture is inconsequential. So we do well to note the exhortation Paul offers to those who possess the gift of showing mercy: "He who shows mercy, [let him exercise his gift] with cheerfulness" (Ro 12:8, NASB). Matthew Henry writes:

> A pleasing countenance in acts of mercy is a great relief and comfort to the miserable; when they see it is not done grudgingly and unwillingly, but with pleasant looks and gentle words, and all possible indications of readiness and alacrity.[3]

The significance of the accompanying "cheerfulness" is seen by Cranfield to be

> evidence of the special charisma that marks a person out for this particular service; but an inward *hilarotes* in ministering will in any case come naturally to one who knows the secret that in those needy and suffering people whom he is called to tend the Lord is Himself present (cf. Mt 25:31 ff.).[4]

In the first century, as now, the gift should probably not be relegated to the comfort of physical distress alone. Especially in the chaotic civilization of today can we see ample instances in which this gift can minister to those who are distressed in mind and spirit as well as body. And the dimension of cheer is so important because the type of service (dealing with the sick and distraught) tends to reflect depression rather than joy. Hospital visitation is usually not the happy highlight of a Christian's week, but he dare not let it become mere duty, or worse, drudgery.

The word *hilarotes* (cheerfulness) is the one from which we get our English words hilarious and hilarity. The contexts of this and other appearances of the word suggest the meaning of joy and cheer, certainly *not* a connotation of humor and mirth at the plight of the sick and needy.

Remember that one of the tests of a spiritual gift is the experience of joy in its use. The person who truly has the gift of showing mercy can also tap the Holy Spirit's reserve of love and joy for his ministry to needy hearts. Grossman suggests:

> Many people shrink from the ill and weak; they consign these problems to an institution. In this area of daily life, mercy is a rare virtue. Wherever a person has this gift, he is a great hope for sick and neglected people. To be sure, merciful persons are quickly besieged by those in need. For this very reason it is important for all who have this talent to use it.[5]

It seems worthy of our notice that no less than four out of the seven *charismata* mentioned in Romans 12: 6-8 deal with practical ministry to needy people, an eloquent testimony to the *service* nature of the Church and the *service* function of spiritual gifts.

12

THE GIFT OF MINISTERING

A FEW WEEKS AGO I was sitting at the front of our church with the other deacons, waiting for a young couple to come forward and be welcomed into membership. As the pastor called their names and they stood, suddenly one of our women, seated across the aisle and three or four rows ahead of them, left her seat. She walked over to the couple, took their small daughter from the mother, and cared for her back in the lobby while the parents came to the front.

A small act to be sure. But typical, I think, of this woman's service to our congregation, and representative of the gift of ministering—or helps, or service. Expressive in a multitude of forms, this gift is plasma in the lifeblood of our churches.

Two words in the original text of Scripture refer to the gift of ministering: *diakonia* in Romans 12:7 and *antilempsis* in 1 Corinthians 12:28. Because different Greek terms are used, it is tempting to wonder whether two separate gifts might be in view. But the proximity which the words have to the other terms for gifts in the two passages, and their very similar definitions, seem to present a focus upon one gift.

Kittel suggests that *antilempsis* is an obvious reference "to the activity of love in the dealings of the community."[1] And of *diakonia* he writes, it is "any discharge of service in genuine love."[2]

The latter term is deliberately broad in scope and indicates how wrong we have been to refer only to pastors as "ministers" and to speak of "entering the ministry" as a narrow occupational choice for very few Christians. Certainly pastors are "ministers." And so are deacons and trustees, teachers and superintendents, choir members and ushers, visitors and youth directors, nursery helpers and custodians.

The first deacons got their name from the word *diakonia* and their task was to minister at tables while the apostles ministered in teaching. It would not be improper to say that both groups of men were engaged in "food service."

This gift of ministering, or helps, represents the quintessential cocoon in which all the other more specialized gifts are contained. Jesus told His disciples that this is the very essence of New Testament leadership: "Let him who is the greatest among you become as the youngest, and the leader as the servant . . . . I am among you as the one who serves" (Lk 22:26-27, NASB).

We know that ministering is the work of all the saints because God says so in Ephesians 4:12. The church officers mentioned in verse 11 have as their task the furnishing of believers in order that they may minister.

*Antilempsis** comes from the verb *antilambanesthai* which, in the middle voice, means "to take a burden on oneself." It is so used in Romans 8:26 (NASB): "the Spirit also helps our weakness," and in Acts 20:35 (NASB): "by working hard in this manner you must help the weak." There is no office or authority in view and no permanence or perpetuation of the particular act of helping.† Very few cults grow up around people who exercise the gift of helps!

---

*The noun form appears only here in the entire New Testament.
†Calvin repudiates this general view and prefers to think of *antilempsis* as "an office, as well as gift, that was exercised in ancient times, but of which we have at this day no knowledge whatever" (*Commentaries on the Epistles of Paul the Apostle to the Corinthians* [Edinburgh: Calvin Translation Society, 1947], 1:416.)

Some commentators refer the gift of ministering to a specific office (perhaps that of deacon) because *diakonia* appears in the list of Romans 12 in a somewhat formal way. Shedd abruptly states that the meaning is to be taken "in the restricted sense of the diaconate [because] the writer is enumerating particular gifts and offices in the church."[3] But surely one sees no basis for an office of giving or showing mercy as these gifts are mentioned in verse 8! We need to guard against our Western cultural tendency to fit everything into a formal bureaucratic pattern.

In comparing and uniting the various services indicated by the two terms we see the breadth and scope of "church ministry":‡

Acts 20:35—Helping the weak
1 Timothy 6:2—Slaves serving Christian owners
Romans 16:3, 9—General assistance in ministry
Ephesians 4:12—Teaching and edifying the church
Acts 6:1-6—Caring for food needs of widows
Romans 15:26-33—Sending an offering to other Christians
Luke 22:27—Serving tables
2 Corinthians 4:1-6—Communicating the Gospel to the lost
Acts 1:17—Being an apostle
Luke 10:40—Serving a guest in your home

This concept of Christian service as ministering to other people appears in all four of the major listings of spiritual gifts.§ In 1 Peter 4 it is so beautifully direct: "Minister [your gifts] . . . one to another, as good stewards of the manifold grace of God" (v. 10). Cranfield talks about the gift of ministering as "the spiritual capacity for practical service" and says that believers should "give themselves

---

‡The list is by no means exhaustive.
§Ro 12; 1 Co 12; Eph 4; 1 Pe 4.

wholeheartedly to the fulfillment of the tasks to which their particular endowment is also their divine vocation."[4]

Perhaps the secret of ministry to others is found in the very wording of Romans 12:7. There is no verb in the Greek text, and in the King James Version words have been supplied to support the emphasis: "Ministry . . . ministering." The idea seems to be, "Don't talk about it, do it." And perhaps what marks those among us who possess this gift is a less-talk-more-action style of service to others, and therefore, of course, to Christ.

13

THE GIFT OF MIRACLES

"I BELIEVE IN MIRACLES," writes John W. Peterson in a song with those words as its title, "for I believe in God." Surely we all agree with Mr. Peterson that the God of the Bible is a God of miracles. The question at stake in a study of the gift of miracles, however, is whether or not that God chooses in this day to perform His miracles through the intermediate instrumentality of man.

The specific terminology in 1 Corinthians 12:10 is *energemata dunameon*—"workings of power." Not every healing is a miracle nor is every miracle a healing (cf. the blinding of Elymas in Acts 13:8-12). And the word *dunamis* does not always refer to a supernatural *physical* manifestation of power. The Gospel, for example, is a spiritual power producing salvation (Ro 1:16), but is thereby no less an evidence of supernatural power.

And we might remind ourselves that not all supernatural power comes from God. The Antichrist will possess "all power and signs and false wonders" (2 Th 2:9, NASB), a most interesting parallel to Hebrews 2:4 (NASB), which tells us that the apostles furthered the message of God while He established their witness "by signs and wonders and by various miracles."

In keeping with our definition and purpose of spiritual gifts, only those "workings of power" which serve to edify the Church are considered spiritual gifts. Obviously

57

evidences of Satan's power would be excluded, as would general pre-Church miracles such as those performed by Moses, Elijah, or even Jesus Himself.

Nevertheless, it is impossible to draw sharp lines of demarcation between Christ and the apostles or between Christ and the Church. We continue His work in the world as the extension of His Body. The same resurrection power of which He partook is in some way available for our use.

But how? In what way? Can we see any evidence that the gift of the working of miracles is possible in the twentieth century? Or must we conclude with some that this and other gifts ceased at the end of the first century?

Again, let me say that dogmatism and closed-mindedness constitute unattractive postures for Christians who serve a God unlimited by the prohibitions of His own creation. The very definition of miracles denotes a supernatural intervention (in the case of a spiritual gift, an intervention of God) into the ordinary course of nature, changing or manipulating physical or spiritual elements to suit His will at a point in time.

The emphasis is always on the Source of the power—the worker is an implement in the hands of God. Godet puts it well: "The persons on whom these gifts are bestowed, not having any importance in themselves, do not count, so to speak."[1]

What were some of the miracles (other than healings) which were a part of the life of the early Church in Acts? We find judgment on unfaithful Christians (5:5-11); exorcism of demons (8:6-7); resurrections from the dead (9:36-42) and deliverances from danger (28:1-6).

Do any Christians today show a supernatural power from the Holy Spirit to raise people from the dead? I do not know. Even if we scale down reports from the Indonesian revivals, there are some rather persistent cases which defy natural explanation.

Is there evidence of genuine exorcism today? I do not know. But a missionary friend of mine, who is hardly given to wild or fanciful exaggerations of his ministry, testifies that God has used him in this way. Another highly respected pastor in a fine evangelical denomination reports similar experiences.

Is it ever possible that God gives a jungle missionary a unique and clearly supernatural power to shake off diseases and dangers which threaten his very survival? I do not know. But Paul's experience with the poisonous snake on Malta surely has some parallels today.

Some will argue that a suggestion of the possibility of the gift of miracles being operative today will open the door to an endless parade of charlatans, to say nothing of those who exercise Satan's power. To be sure, that danger is real! But no more real than the opportunity for Marjoe to bilk unsuspecting thousands of their money through an unscrupulous peddling of a quasi gift of evangelism.

We dare not be guided in our understanding of spiritual gifts by a fear born of unhappy experiences nor an exegesis which results from hermeneutical myopia. Of course, such a rule holds true to the positive evidences of any gift as well. The only dependable criterion is the text of God's truth itself. And there seems to be no portion of Scripture which offers a clear statement that the gift of miracles ever completely ceased in the Church or, if it did, that God could not restore it in any age in which He chose to do so. Remember, too, that spiritual miracles are just as much the workings of power as their more dramatic physical counterparts.

14

THE GIFT OF PASTORING

THE CHURCH is the ongoing work of Jesus Christ in the world. As such, its use of spiritual gifts is reflective of our Lord's own earthly ministry. No doubt He possessed every spiritual gift in its most perfect form, though we do not have a record of His exercise of them all. Some of the gifts are uniquely reminiscent of the incarnate Word— teaching, prophesying, showing mercy, and certainly shepherding.*

The Greek word from which we derive the concept of a pastor-shepherd ministry is *poimen*, whose root meaning denotes protection and care. We call the shepherd of a church "pastor" from the Latin translation of *poimen* (*pastores*). Only in Ephesians 4:11 are congregational leaders called shepherds, although the idea of the shepherd-leader in the church appears frequently in the New Testament (Jn 21:16; Ac 20:28; 1 Pe 5:2).

Some commentators link the terms *pastor-teacher* because of the different grammatical structure in the latter part of the verse. Perhaps they are influenced by the necessity for pastors to be able to teach (1 Ti 3:2; Titus 1:9), but we may not be under any ultimate exegetical demand to tie the two together. On the other hand there certainly are some mutual responsibilities. Foulkes puts it this way:

> Apostles and evangelists had a particular task in planting the church in every place, prophets for bringing a

---

*Jn 10; Heb 13:20; 1 Pe 2:25.

particular word from God to a situation. Pastors and teachers were gifted to be responsible for the day-to-day building up of the church. There is no hard and fast line to be drawn between the two.[1]

In focusing on Ephesians 4:11 we see again the need for distinguishing between gifts and offices. The five items identified in this verse describe gifted leaders, already given gifts by the Spirit, now given to the Church by Christ. In each case an office as well as a gift seems to be implied. With the office of pastor comes accompanying authority and responsibility in the congregation, but not to the point of autocracy, as Peter clearly warns (1 Pe 5:1-4).

The very analogy of one who cares for a flock leads us to an understanding of the multiple facets of this gift. The pastor is to guard the flock from its enemies so as to preserve it from destruction from within and without. But the protective function of a shepherd is only part of the task. He must also teach, lead, feed, and prepare refreshing rest for his charges. It is also his responsibility to seek the lost, redirect the straying, heal the wounds of the sick, and blend the members into unity and mutuality.

And far from creating a dependence upon himself, it is rather the pastor's duty to lead the flock to ministry (Eph 4:12), to equip them to serve Christ by serving each other, and to build a capacity for self-preservation and self-edification.

Note that the first three gifts listed in verse 11 refer more to the universal Church and the last two to the local church as we know it. This is not to say that such a specific division was clear in the first century, but rather that it has evolved in later years of the Church. Lange points out:

> Little good has ever resulted from the attempt to reproduce accurately as *jure divirio* those distinctions which expositors discover in the offices of the primitive

church. It may be remarked that while this phrase shows that every pastor ought to be a teacher, putting the former phase of duty first, it will ever be the case that through native endowment some ministers are better adapted for one part of the duty than for the other, though there is no warrant for total neglect of either.[2]

Let it be noted that the gift of pastoral care is a ministry to people beyond the level of teaching them. There is implied a dimension of patience, an attitude of long-suffering not essential to the ministry of teaching in, let us say, a seminary noncongregational setting. To be sure, there is an element of pastoring in any teaching, and the teacher who applies it in the Spirit greatly enhances his ministry.

It is encouraging to see the gift of pastoral ministry being developed with enthusiasm again in the mid-1970s. Toward the end of the last decade the Church experienced a "low" in self-concept. The constant attacks of the sixties had taken their toll, and discouragement was rampant. But now veteran pastors seem more optimistic regarding what Christ is doing in His Church. And potential pastors are cramming evangelical seminaries at a rate unprecedented in the modern era.

And seminary students today are anxious for the people-developing type of ministry which biblical pastoring calls for. As Mains testifies:

> It is no longer enough for me, as a pastor, to feel satisfied with a solitary display of my gift. My ministry must include assisting each one in our congregation to find expression for his particular gift or gifts.[3]

So in addition to whatever else it may be, the gift of pastoring is a catalyst geared toward releasing the potential of other gifts. It could well be also that the Holy Spirit, knowing the vast and diverse tasks of congregational care, equips pastors with several gifts to enable them to minister effectively as the undershepherds among Christ's flock.

15

THE GIFT OF PROPHECY

THE CHURCH AT CORINTH was planted during the second missionary journey immediately after Paul left Athens. Corinth was one of the most wicked cities of its day, so much so that the term *Corinthian* came to be synonymous with immorality and sex perversion. Awareness of the nature of the city helps us in understanding the church to which Paul wrote two epistles, and an understanding of the church is most strategic in grasping Paul's emphasis on the use of the gift of prophecy in the congregation there. After listing the spiritual gifts in great detail, and relating them to the unity of the Body of Christ (1 Co 12), Paul pauses to emphasize how all spiritual gifts must be administered in an attitude and atmosphere of love (1 Co 13). Then, in an immediate transition, chapter 14 begins with these words:

> Let love be your greatest aim; nevertheless, ask also for the special abilities the Holy Spirit gives, and especially the gift of prophecy, being able to preach the messages of God (TLB).

In 14:20 the apostle suggests that the genuinely mature Christian should understand the significance of prophecy and its relationship to tongues, and that such understanding is the mark of spiritual adulthood. Never one to miss an opportunity for practical application, Paul indicates that the wise Christian will be naive concerning evil but should be most mature concerning the issues of the Christian life, specifically in this instance of spiritual gifts. He warns that one does not examine evil even in the worthy name of "research," but learns what he needs to know about evil from God's Word itself rather than by dabbling in various kinds of sin, the occult, and similar areas in the domain of Satan.

The word *propheteia* comes from the verb *prophēmi*, which means "to speak forth." When defining any word of Scripture, one must take into consideration two extremely important factors: *etymology* (the basic derivation of the word) and *use*. Sometimes they are greatly different, and most scholars would agree that use at the time of the word's appearance takes precedence in determining its meaning. In this case, however, there is no great difference between the deriviation of the word and its use. The idea of speaking forth, particularly speaking forth the Word of God, is common in all the appearances. The problem comes when we link New Testament with Old Testament usage. In the latter, the prophet was primarily a foreteller whose task and ministry it was to proclaim future events before they happened. That aspect of the word is not absent from New Testament usage but, as the great Greek scholar Rudolph Kittel suggests, the idea of prediction in the word is really a "special sense" and one which "occurs chiefly in Revelation."[1]

Even early in the New Testament, prophecy was largely personal inspiration as God's revelation came directly to men like Peter and Paul. But as the gift began to be used with regularity in the established congregations, it quickly became more of an analysis of written revelation. A. T. Robertson refers to it as "speaking forth God's message under the guidance of the Holy Spirit."[2] If I were to attempt a short and understandable definition, it would probably sound something like this: "The gift of prophecy is congregational preaching which explains and applies God's revelation."

Indeed, we could say that prophecy is of *primary* importance with respect to the public ministry of the Church. Paul is very clear in 1 Corinthians 14 (NASB): "Desire ... that you may prophesy" (v. 1); "I wish that you all spoke in tongues, but even more that you would prophesy" (v. 5); and "Therefore, my brethren, desire earnestly to prophesy" (v. 39). In 12:28 he lists the role of the prophet immediately after the role of the apostle in the hierarchy of importance for the ministry of the Church.

There is, of course, a very practical reason for all of this. Prophecy produces the kind of results which are absolutely necessary if we are to have spiritually equipped and mature Christians in our churches. Verse 3 of chapter 14 is the clue: "But he that prophesieth speaketh unto men to edification, and exhortation, and comfort." It took me a long time to realize how many times the idea of edification (upbuilding spiritual growth) is mentioned in this chapter. It is virtually a dominating theme appearing with emphasis in verses 3, 4, 5, 12, 17, and 26. Indeed, one might very well say that chapter 14 of 1 Corinthians is *not primarily about tongues or prophecy, but rather about an edificational ministry in the Church.*

The word *exhortation* basically means "encouragement" and, of course, the concept "comfort" is quite clear. All of these three are much-needed elements in the contemporary Church. We have many discouraged Christians who need encouragement. We have millions of people who are flocking to the offices of counselors, psychologists, and psychiatrists in search of peace and comfort in exceedingly troubled times. We have entire congregations of people starving spiritually because their weekly diet contains insufficient edificational calories to sustain any decent measure of spiritual health. Exercise of the gift of prophecy was not only important to the church of Corinth in the first century; it is a pressing need in the evangelical church of today!

Tongues are used as a sign to those who do not believe the Gospel. Prophecy, on the other hand, is not primarily aimed at the unsaved, but rather at people who have already trusted Christ and are members of the family of God through regeneration. This is also one of the major differences between prophetic preaching and evangelistic preaching. Evangelistic preaching centers on the basic gospel of salvation by faith in Christ through the grace of God, whereas prophetic preaching deals with the total revelation of God. Evangelistic preaching is geared to the unsaved and is, in that sense, very definitely missionary in scope. Prophetic preaching, on the other hand, is aimed at saved people and exercised in the gatherings of the community of the redeemed which we call local churches.

Since prophetic preaching deals with the *total* revelation of God, it also deals with the essential elements of the Gospel, and for that reason can be at times evangelistic. That is not its primary purpose, however, but merely a fringe benefit. In verse 24 the apostle says:

> But if you prophesy, preaching God's Word [even though such preaching is for believers] and an unsaved person or a new Christian comes in who does not understand about these things, all these sermons will convince him of the fact that he is a sinner, and his conscience will be pricked by everything he hears. As he listens, his secret thoughts will be laid bare and he will fall down on his knees and worship God, declaring that God is really there among you (TLB).

Prophetic preaching is evangelistic because it produces *conviction, judgment,* and *spiritual awareness.* It is quite common in our day to see people who are really born again become disenchanted with their attendance at liberal churches where there is no solid prophetic preaching. Because they have not been fed, they are still "unlearned" in the things of God's revelation even though they may have been Christians for a number of years. Invariably, the thing that attracts them to a vital evangelical congregation is not the building, the program, or even the friendliness of the people, but rather their hunger for expository preaching.

The Plymouth Brethren have been telling us for a long time that most of the rest of us in main-line denominations have missed the point of the New Testament's emphasis on multiple ministry. Though their lack of form may have become a form in itself, they offer a handle on New Testament patterns that we have not been willing to admit. Total involvement of God's people in ministry is certainly the desired end result of the development and use of spiritual gifts. In terms of prophecy, we tend to identify only one congregational preacher, and the rest of us become resigned to audience behavior. However, our chapter does say, "Let the prophets speak *two* or *three*" (v. 29) and even "but if *all* prophesy" (v. 24). One cannot very easily pass over the multiple emphasis.

It seems that in the seventies more congregations are experimenting with alternatives to the one-man pulpit. The sharing of the preaching ministry with others who have the gift of prophesy is a valid New Testament option, and the allowing of response to preaching seems to be well in line with the end of verse 29: "Let the other judge."

In recognizing the multiple nature of the exercise of the gift of prophecy, we see that the gift is under the rational control of the individual prophet. To be specific, utterances do not come pouring ecstatically out of a man as he sits in the seventeenth pew at the Sunday evening service. I like the way *The Living Bible* renders verse 32: "Remember that a person who has a message from God has the power to stop himself or wait his turn." Multiple ministry in the utilization of the gift of prophecy is not confusion, noise, or pandemonium. It is logical, quiet, and orderly speaking. Otherwise, it does not emanate from God (v. 33).

What about the question of women prophets? There is

no doubt in the New Testament that women had the gift of prophecy. Philip's daughters, for example, exercised the gift at home. And that is the clue. Although women may have the gift of prophecy, there seems to be no New Testament precedent for having them exercise that gift *in the congregation*. It is possible that Paul's words in verse 34—"Let your women keep silence in the churches"—refers to the use of the two gifts of prophecy and tongues, although some reputable commentators suggest an application to the disruptive chatter of women in the synagogues.

I take the position that ordination of women is an antibiblical idea. Women, on the other hand, may indeed have the gift of prophecy, and they may exercise it in many other avenues, such as ministry at home, in Bible classes, and, of course, in the Sunday school. The reason for all of this seems to be that exercising the gift of prophecy in the corporate congregational life of the Church would tend to violate the prior principle of submissiveness and obedience. Indeed, this is precisely the contrast that Paul makes in verses 34 and 35.

The results of the proper use of the gift of prophecy in the modern congregation will not be greatly different than the results in the first century. Congregational life will take on order, peace, and the general benefits of the exercise of this important gift: exhortation, comfort, conviction, spiritual awareness, learning, but, above all, edification—the primary task of the gathered church.

16

THE GIFT OF TEACHING

JUST AS THE GIFT of pastoring reminds us of the earthly shepherding ministry of the Lord Jesus, so an appreciation of the gift of teaching should lead us to think about Jesus as the master Teacher.

The one who exercises the gift of teaching in the church is one who follows in the pattern of Christ feeding His body. In looking at some of the spiritual gifts, it seems to be more difficult to understand their relationship to the collective Body of Christ in congregation, although I have tried to show that relationship in dealing with each gift. The communal context for the exercise of gifts is basic, and one can certainly see how the gift of teaching is of significant importance in the total role of the edification of the Church, the ultimate goal of all gifts.

Howard A. Snyder warns against "the tendency to over-individualize spiritual gifts" when he says:

> Western Christianity in general has tended to over-individualize the gospel to the detriment of its more communal and collective aspects, and contemporary conceptions of spiritual gifts have suffered from this tendency. Spiritual gifts are too often thought of as strictly a matter of one's "private" relationship to God, without regard for the Christian community. In contrast, Paul repeatedly emphasizes that the Spirit's gifts are for the edification of the church, and that they lose their significance if this emphasis is lost.[1]

The gift of teaching is mentioned in three out of the four major passages dealing with spiritual gifts (Ro 12:7; 1 Co 12:28-29; Eph 4:11). In the Romans passage Paul emphasizes that the one who teaches is to see his gift as a service to the community and to exercise it in relation to those who make up the Body. The same kind of communal emphasis appears in 1 Corinthians 12, especially since the reference to "teachers" appears after the elongated section dealing with the unity-in-diversity which is the Body of Christ. In the Ephesians passage, the context again is clearly the Church, both universal (as the earlier verses of the chapter clearly specify) and local, in view of the fact that this epistle is being written to a local church at Ephesus.

However, in the Ephesians passage there is also the implication of a sense of office since the word *didaskaloi* appears in line with the other officers mentioned in the verse. As indicated earlier, the concept of "pastors and teachers" (v. 11) could be understood either as two separate offices or as a description of "pastors who teach." Whichever interpretation one prefers, he cannot escape the fact that in the other two passages teaching is a distinctly different gift than pastoring.

MacPherson treats the Ephesians passage in an interesting way and draws a distinction I have not seen discussed in any other place. After indicating that the teacher is one who has been charged with the task of "imparting doctrinal instruction," he goes on to suggest that this office

> is the Christian equivalent of the Jewish "rabbi." The work of the pastor was to follow up in his own more limited sphere that of the apostle; the work of the teacher was to follow up in a systematic way the work of the prophet. "If the prophet," says Godet on 1 Corinthians 12:28, "may be compared to the traveler who discovers new countries, the teacher is like the geographer who combines the scattered results of these discoveries and gives a methodological statement of them."[2]

The concept of the *didaskalos* (teacher) is a common but important one in the New Testament. Kittel tells us that it occurs fifty-eight times, forty-eight of which are in the gospels. And of those usages in the gospels, forty-one times the word refers to Jesus and only seven to others.[3] The apostle Paul applied the term to himself in 1 Timothy 2:7 and 2 Timothy 1:11. Of course these are just the references to the noun form, not including the many other references to the process of teaching.

I have attempted to make a distinction between the prophet in Old Testament times and in New Testament times, and the use of the gift of prophecy in the Church today. It is clear that both Old Testament prophets and, to a lesser extent, New Testament prophets engaged in a revelational ministry. That is, they communicated direct truth from God, revealed to them in lieu of written revelation on the subject. As I see it, modern-day exercise of the gift of prophecy is nonrevelational but rather explanatory and applicatory in form.

In contrast, the gift of teaching seems to have always been explanatory and applicatory. The rabbis based their teaching both upon the Old Testament Scriptures and upon the Talmud and Mishna. New Testament teachers obviously explained the Messianic character of the Old Testament with particular application to Jesus of Nazareth. Today the gift of teaching is much the same as it always has been among God's people. It focuses upon written revelation and seeks to show how that revelation is understandable and relevant in any given age. It would seem that the major difference between the gift of teaching in the New Testament church and the gift of teaching today is that the teacher today has the completed canon of Scripture to deal with and also nineteen centuries of Church history to shed light upon his hermeneutical task. There seems to be a clear implication of study, mental and verbal skills, and reliance upon the Holy Spirit in the ministry of teaching.

Jesus promised that when the Spirit came to the disciples He would "guide you into all the truth; for He will not speak on His own initiative, but whatever He hears, He will speak; and He will disclose to you what is to come" (Jn 16:13, NASB). A reference to their recording of the New Testament Scriptures? Yes, that surely was included. But limiting that promise only to the inspiration of the New Testament text seems to me to do damage to the phrase "into all the truth." Surely the principle of the Spirit's guidance in teaching can be claimed by any Sunday school teacher or pastor in our day just as it could be claimed by the men who wrote the New Testament canon. I like the way Shedd suggests that the gift of teaching implies "the common knowledge of a devout and disciplined Christian mind."[4]

Every evangelical church is committed to teaching in some form. Though a few churches have experimented with substitutes, the traditional Sunday school is still very popular among Evangelicals, and there are indications that it is rebounding from a downward trend at the end of the last decade and the beginning of this. Consequently we do well to focus again upon the teaching ministry of the church. Rather than just trying to "fill jobs" in the Sunday school with any warm and willing bodies, it certainly behooves church leaders to examine people's spiritual gifts to see whether we can staff our Sunday schools with people who have the gift of teaching.

It may very well be that not every Sunday school teacher has the gift of teaching, nor should have. As in evangelism, there are those who are responsible for ministering in the same arena as that covered by a spiritual gift (every Christian having the responsibility for sharing his faith). To be very specific, all Christians have some responsibility for teaching as they mature in the faith, but not every Christian has the gift of teaching.

Nevertheless, we certainly want to do what we can to identify and press into important service those believers among us whom the Holy Spirit has chosen to equip with the gift of teaching. Robertson and Plummer speak to the distinction between general teaching and gift teaching in a very helpful paragraph from their commentary on 1 Corinthians:

> Men whose natural powers and acquired knowledge were augmented by a special gift. It is evident from "Are all teachers?" (v. 29) that there was a class of teachers to which only some Christians belonged, and the questions which follow show that "teachers," like "workers of miracles," were distinguished by the possession of some gift. In Ephesians 4:11 we are not sure whether "pastors and teachers" means one class or two, but at any rate it is probable that whereas "apostles," "prophets," and "evangelists" instructed both the converted and the unconverted, "pastors and teachers" ministered to settled congregations.[5]

One further note of importance is found in the epistle of James. James 3:1 suggests that one can choose whether he wants to be a teacher or not, and every Christian ought to be careful about selecting a position of this importance. Surely in an effort to be consistent with the rest of the New Testament, we would have to recognize that such a personal choice would be based upon a person's awareness of possessing the gift of teaching. When one does recognize that gift in himself, he has the responsibility of thanking God for it, seeking to develop it, and using it for the edification of the body.

Dr. Roy Zuck points out that there are only three reasons for poor teaching in the church: "If teachers are ineffective, either they do not have the teaching gift, or are not developing it, or are not in fellowship with the Lord."[6]

17

THE GIFT OF TONGUES

THERE IS NO ISSUE so controversial and divisive in evangelical Christianity today as the issue of tongues. And it is not one that is likely to go away soon. Dr. Kenneth Kantzer suggests, "The last third of twentieth century church history may well become remembered as 'The Revival of Charismatic Gifts.' "[1] Total world membership in Pentecostal bodies is estimated at over ten million, and Kantzer suggests that when charismatics within mainline Protestant denominations are added to that total it is surely safe to say "that the actual figures for those who claim to have spoken in tongues or who regularly participate in meetings where the gift is honored and practiced as a normal experience for the church today, probably run much higher than those that have been cited."

Articles and books on the gift of tongues abound, and there is surely no need in this book for more opinion on the subject. The following paragraphs therefore will attempt to do just two things: to help the reader sort out the crucial questions that must be asked for an intelligent understanding of the issue; and, to indicate one more time the significant passages of Scripture which give us information on the subject.

Actually the question, What is the gift of tongues? only gives rise to several others. It becomes immediately essential to identify the nature of the gift of tongues in each of the instances in which it appears in Scripture and then to make a comparative judgment between the biblical gift and that practiced by the contemporary charismatic movement. The options in each case are essentially two: either the gift of tongues enabled men to speak in unlearned languages, or it produced an ability to speak in ecstatic utterances. Though there are strong opinions on each side, the weight of evidence certainly seems to lean toward an interpretation of tongues as unlearned languages, both in the three crucial Acts passages* and in the experience of the Corinthian church.†

The word in question is the Greek word *glōssa*. It is clearly the word for "language," and only a unique contextual interpretation would lead one to the conclusion that the reference is to ecstatic utterance. Yet Dr. Charles Smith, after fifteen pages of examination of the texts, concludes:

> All the evidence suggests that biblical tongues were in all cases ecstatic utterances and essentially unintelligible. Any such utterances (today as well) may occasionally have included foreign words or phrases, but these were only bits and pieces in the mass of unrecognizable sounds.[2]

A more common view is suggested by Walvoord, who says, "Any view which denies that speaking in tongues used actual languages is difficult to harmonize with the Scriptural concept of a spiritual gift."[3]

Some attempt to make a distinction between the Acts passages and the 1 Corinthians passage, indicating that in Acts the speakers did indeed use languages, but at Corinth the gift had degenerated into meaningless ecstatic utterance. Sometimes 1 Corinthians 14:2 is advanced as evidence ("in the spirit he speaketh mysteries"). But the crucial question at Corinth seemed to be that some were

*Ac 2:1-42; 10:1-48; 19:1-7.
†1 Co 12-14.

using the gift without interpretation, in the absence of which a tongue becomes an unknown mystery which no one understands. Kittel puts it this way:

> The uncontrolled use of tongues might thus make it appear that the community is an assembly of madmen (14:23, 27). Yet tongues are a legitimate sign of overwhelming power (14:22). There are various kinds (12:10, 28; cf. 14:10); some are tongues of men and others of angels (13:1). To make *glossolalia* serviceable to the community, however, either the speaker or another brother must be able to give an interpretation (14:5, 13, 27 f; 12:10, 30). In Corinth, therefore, *glossolalia* is an unintelligible ecstatic utterance.[4]

It seems to me that any attempts to make *glossa* mean something different in 1 Corinthians than it does in the book of Acts are suspect and rest upon very fragile evidence.

But still we have the question of whether *contemporary* tongues are ecstatic utterance or languages. Certainly if one concludes that the biblical gift is exclusively a reference to speaking in unlearned languages, persons who claim to have the gift of tongues and yet claim ecstatic utterance would fail to qualify as possessing the genuine article. At this point, of course, the argument goes back to the charismatic movement demonstrating in some way that contemporary tongues are languages. Some have called for scientific investigation, such as the offer by those who have the gift to allow linguists to examine its properties. I am not convinced scientific investigation is ever the best approach to judging spiritual value, however, and in some cases (such as the matter of personal salvation) such corroboration would be virtually impossible.

Gundry claims that if we subtracted all the tongues speakers who admit to using ecstatic utterance rather than unlearned languages, "most claims to *glossolalia* could be rejected on this basis alone."[5] I am not sure that statement could be supported, but certainly the issue of recognizing what tongues are or are not is a crucial one.

Those particularly interested in researching further the issue of contemporary *glossolalia* will want to check William J. Samarin's book *Tongues of Men and Angels.*[6] Samarin is a Christian linguist whose research in the area of modern tongues speakers has convinced him that contemporary tongues are basically not languages. But then Samarin also concludes that the tongues referred to in 1 Corinthians were not real languages, either, since he believes the early Christians practiced ecstatic utterance in much the same way that it is used by present-day charismatics. So after a quick wheel around the circle, we are back where we started.

One could reasonably assume that God's purpose in giving the gift of tongues initially carries through to the use of contemporary tongues if they are a demonstration of the spiritual gift. Perhaps it is important at the outset in attempting to answer this question that we recognize what the gift of tongues is *not*. There is no evidence in Scripture that the gift of tongues is the signal of some special kind of evidence such as the baptism of the Holy Spirit. It is diametrically opposed to the very nature of the sovereign issuing of spiritual gifts that any one gift should be normative for all Christians or that it should represent some high level of spiritual maturity. The very fact that the carnal and divisive congregation at Corinth apparently made ample use of the gift of tongues is indicative that its presence does not denote special spirituality and, conversely, its absence does not denote any lack of spirituality or of special experience which God wants every Christian to have.

The central passage here is 1 Corinthians 12:13, where Paul indicates that all believers have been "baptized into one body." And in verse 30 Paul asks the question, "Do all speak with tongues?" It is obviously rhetorical, anticipating a negative response.

But what was the significance of tongues in the New Testament? Most evangelical commentators agree that the primary purpose was to be a sign. Both in Acts 2 and at Corinth (14:22) the sign was to unbelievers to somehow signify the presence and power of God.

There seems to have been, however, at Corinth an additional use for the gift for purposes of edification. The one who spoke in an unknown tongue without interpretation edified himself (14:4), and the one who spoke in the congregation with an unknown tongue and was followed by an interpreter contributed to the edification of the congregation (14:5, 26).

Still a third purpose for tongues was their use in *prayer* (14:2). In a sense this is the same thing as self-edification indicated above. Stedman argues that the use of tongues in the congregational meetings at all was merely a permission and never the original intention of the gift. Perhaps so, but the regulations of 1 Corinthians 14 clearly indicate that Paul expected the Corinthians to use it in their congregational life and that the benefit of it was not merely for unbelievers, as Stedman intimates,[7] since one does not edify an unbeliever, and edification was apparently possible at Corinth if tongues were exercised in the proper way.

With various subcategories and nuances of interpretation and application, it would appear that there are generally three categories into which one's analysis of the contemporary charismatic movement must fall.

1. Obviously one could admit that this is *a restoration to the Church in these latter days of a genuine spiritual gift*, again for purposes of sign and edification. One does not have to be openly enthusiastic about the charismatic movement to agree with Ryrie's caution when he writes, "What about tongues today? One cannot say that God would never give this gift or other of the limited gifts today."[8] Ryrie does go on to suggest that he believes the gift ceased "with the production of the written Word"

which, of course, is the standard dispensational interpretation. It seems to me, however, that the evidence so frequently offered (namely that 1 Co 13:8-10 indicates that tongues ceased with the appearance of the completed canon of Scripture which is to be equated with "that which is perfect") does irreparable damage to the context of that chapter.

I am not arguing for open acceptance of the movement, but at least an open-mindedness toward the views of other believers. Scriptures will scarcely support the conclusion that this option is closed because the gift ceased at the end of the first century. The frightening dogmatism of Smith is almost cultic in its rigid closed-mindedness: "When tongues ceased, they ceased. Since the Apostolic Age the Holy Spirit has not and will not again cause people to speak in tongues."⁹

2. A second possibility is that tongues-speaking as we know it today is indeed *supernatural in the sense that it is satanic*. Certainly Satan has an unchallengeable reputation as one who seeks to forge his own replica of every major thing God has tried to do. There is no reason why he should not have false tongues-speakers in the same way that he has had false prophets down through the ages. While recognizing this as a real possibility, the discretion of Gundry is well taken when he says, "We would prefer to think that such cases are rare and should leave the judgement to God unless the indications are perfectly clear."¹⁰

3. A third position of explanation gaining in popularity is the suggestion that tongues-speaking is *primarily a psychological experience*. It could be self-induced through the forced repetition of unintelligible expressions or some form of subconscious temporary euphoria which looks to be spiritual ecstacy. Quite obviously tongues-speaking could be psychological. Indeed, when some leaders in the charismatic movement advertise books and tapes which teach persons how to produce nonsense syllables with the

intent of learning to speak in tongues, it is easy to see how this explanation could account for a reasonably large segment of those engaged in the phenomenon. The possibility of a psychologized state should cause us to be careful in attributing any tongues experience we have occasion to see either to the spiritual gift or to the power of Satan.

It would seem that those Evangelicals who claim to have received the gift of tongues would want to take every precaution toward demonstrating the biblical orientation of their gift. In order to do so, I would think that at least four basic guidelines must be employed:

1. They should openly admit that tongues is not normative of any spiritual experience or any level of spiritual maturity. In other words, a tongues speaker is not thereby shown to be any closer to God than a non-tongues speaker.

2. They should not seek the gift, try to "learn" how to speak in tongues, nor try to teach anyone else to speak in tongues. Certainly one learns *how to use* spiritual gifts such as teaching and evangelism, but that seems to be a considerably different thing than learning *how to get* a spiritual gift. The latter is patently unbiblical since spiritual gifts are given purely in the sovereignty of the Holy Spirit.

3. They should not seek to force the reception of this gift on any other person any more than one would force the gifts of teaching, evangelism, or helps on other Christians.

4. They should always exercise the gift according to the clear rules of 1 Corinthians 14:

a. Tongues speaking should be done toward the goal of edification (v. 26).

b. There should never be more than three in a service (v. 27).

c. It should never be done without an interpreter (vv. 27-28).

d. The service must be conducted in order, without chaos and confusion (vv. 33, 40).

e. Possibly a prohibition should be placed upon women speaking in tongues in a public service (vv. 34-35). Not all commentators agree that these verses refer to tongue-speaking or prophecy. They may be a criticism of the synagogue "chatter section" whose members apparently disrupted public worship by their obtrusive talking. Nevertheless, when compared with 1 Timothy 2:11-12, this portion of 1 Corinthians 14 at least ought to give us pause in verbal feminine leadership in the local assembly. A glance at the role of women in the history of the cults is an additional vivid lesson.

In conclusion let me suggest several principles which may help us in reaction to tongues speakers with whom we may be acquainted or may guide us in dealing with an incident of tongues-speaking in a church which has never known it before.

We should not:

1. Respond with an emotional and experientially based negation of the movement. Some Evangelicals criticize the tongues movement for its experience orientation and then proceed to attack charismatics by saying, "You should have seen what they did to our church."

2. Interpret it away with questionable exegesis.

3. Attack the tongues speaker or the charismatic movement in bitterness, strife, and intolerance.[11]

4. Make this the big issue of theology and seek confrontation with charismatics just to provoke debate.

We should:

1. Understand the biblical information as clearly as we can through careful Bible study.

2. Insist that charismatics follow the biblical rules for the practice of the gift they claim to have.

3. Show an attitude of love and tolerance in keeping with Paul's suggestion, "forbid not to speak with tongues" (14:39).

4. Take precautions against division and schism in our own churches.

It is my opinion that Evangelicals have been trying to attack a pragmatic problem by theologizing it out of existence. It has not worked. It seems that we can request, and even require, tongues speakers to abide by the biblical guidelines or keep private the gift they claim to exercise. Certainly schools have the right to identify certain rules or prohibitions concerning the use of any gift on campus. And in the church we should recognize the necessity of edification and the unity that spiritual gifts should exemplify.

In a fine article attempting to find a mediating posture such as I have sought, Millard Erickson shares "Paul's great concern regarding the group [for] understanding and communication" and suggests:

> Whether or not we believe the Holy Spirit is bestowing charismatic gifts such as speaking in tongues today, we can be assured that He is at work filling, sanctifying, empowering and guiding believers and producing His fruits. In this we can rejoice. And this we ought to seek.[12]

I agree.

18

THE GIFT OF WISDOM

WISDOM IS a another limitless theme in Scripture. Several books in the Old Testament speak about it in great length, and for centuries it has been one of the most significant religious themes in the Middle East. The very essence of wisdom is consistent with the nature of God, and, like truth, all wisdom finds its ultimate source in the Creator. Furthermore, wisdom is not something which, like doctrine or science, can be taught in a classroom. It is a combined exercise of mind and spirit as the Christian responds to God's guiding and gifting activity in his life.

Wisdom can be accumulated through experience, but this is not true of the "utterance of wisdom" which marks the spiritual gift. As with all spiritual gifts, the gift of wisdom is supernatural, focusing on the meaning or interpretation of truth, producing understanding of solutions to some problem, or offering the application of knowledge to spiritual life.

In chapter 10 on the gift of knowledge, I attempted to make some distinctions between "the utterance of wisdom" and "the utterance of knowledge" since their side-by-side appearance in 1 Corinthians 12:8 certainly requires us to see them as two distinct gifts. Edwards seems to think that there is a unique distinction in 1 Corinthians, apart from the use of *sophia* and *gnosis* as they appear elsewhere in the New Testament.

Their use in this epistle seems to show that *logos sophias* denotes the power of expounding spiritual truths, which it is the gift of the spiritual man, the *teleios*, both to understand and to speak. Its object is revealed truth; its power is the illumination of the spirit; its method a spiritual synthesis; and its results are communicated to others in words taught by the Holy Ghost.[1]

It is significant that the gifts both of wisdom and knowledge are introduced by the phrase, "the word of," implying the practical nature of these spiritual gifts. That is in keeping with what we know about special gifts in general. They are not some ethereal or mystical cultic rites practiced only in secret by the initiated, but rather a demonstration of ministry in action as it served the edification of the Church. Godet is most helpful in understanding the relationship between knowledge and wisdom. Says the great Lutheran writer, "Gnosis makes the teacher; wisdom, the preacher and pastor. When corrupted, the former becomes gnosticism, the speculation of the intellectualist; the latter, dead orthodoxy."[2]

Most commentators agree that we should not make anything of the order in which the spiritual gifts are listed in 1 Corinthians 12:8-10. The prominence of prophecy in chapter 14, for example, would not warrant its being placed sixth in a list, if that list tended to convey importance and value.

At the mention of the idea of "value," I am reminded that wisdom is certainly a gift applied in the development of a Christian system of values. One commentary suggests that wisdom "is the more comprehensive term. By it we know the true value of things through seeing what they really are; it is spiritual insight and comprehension."[3] Incidentally, there is no definite article in the Greek text, but rather the expression "a word of wisdom." Perhaps there is an emphasis here on communication of God's value system to others.

Paul makes a great deal out of the philosophy of the

world and the philosophy of Christ, indicating that the Christian needs to learn how to see things from "divine viewpoint" rather than always being fogged in by the secularistic materialism and humanism of a pagan culture. Perhaps it is the gift of "a word of wisdom" that enables the Christian man to see beyond the smog of earthly intellect to the unique order of priorities in the mind of God (Is 55:8-9).

CONCLUSION

IT IS TIME to wrap some strings around the package. Conclusions need to be drawn, a few generalizations made, and some clarifications offered of concepts that may still be, at this point, somewhat hazy. Furthermore, it may be necessary to reiterate certain important points for emphasis.

Perhaps all of that can best be done by suggesting three sets of four propositions geared to suggest first of all the congregational setting for an understanding of spiritual gifts; second, a review of some basic negations concerning spiritual gifts; and finally, generalizations regarding the use of spiritual gifts in the life of our churches. At the risk of sounding dogmatic and making the generalizations look too broad, I have chosen to begin the three sets of propositions with the words *every, no,* and *all.*

1. *Every believer is a member of the Body of Christ, which is the Church.* We simply cannot separate our understanding of spiritual gifts from the content of 1 Corinthians 12. In Paul's closely drawn analogy of the human body, he seems to suggest that the spiritual gifts enumerated enable the members of the spiritual Body to operate spiritual faculties in the spiritual realm, just as the physical body is able to utilize the operations of its various members in the physical realm. But one does not participate in this activity unless he is a part of the body. On the other hand, it is impossible to be a believer, to genuinely know Jesus Christ in regeneration, and not be a part of the universal Church described with such clarity in this chapter.

2. *Every member of the Church has a place of ministry.*
Ministry (serving) is what spiritual gifts are all about.
Each of the four primary passages makes this very plain
(Ro 12; 1 Co 12; Eph 4; 1 Pe 4). And not only that,
but the ministry of Christ's Body is, in reality, the ministry
of Christ.

3. *Every member of the Body needs every other member of the Body.* I like the way the Amplified Bible phrases
Romans 12:5: "So we, numerous as we are, are one
body in Christ, the Messiah, and individually we are
parts one of another—mutually dependent on one
another."

4. *Every member has at least one spiritual gift.* The
Greek work *ekastō* appears in 1 Corinthians 12:7,11 and is
best translated "to each other." How different our churches
would be if we would all stop either being awed by the
multiple gifts of others or, on the other extreme, being
constantly critical of the way persons use or do not use
their spiritual gifts. Stedman issues the call with clarity:

> Once you realize that God Himself has equipped you
> with a uniquely designed pattern of spiritual gifts and
> has placed you where he wants you in order to minister
> those gifts, you enter into a new dimension of exciting
> possibility. This awaits any true Christian who is willing
> to give time and thought to the discovery and under-
> standing of his pattern of gifts. He must also submit
> himself to the authority of the head of the body, who
> reserves the right to coordinate and direct its activities.[1]

1. *No gift today is revelational in the New Testament
sense.* Although the primary emphasis of Revelation 22:
17-18 is to the text of the Apocalypse itself, the principle
of a completed canon remains and there is no biblical or
experiential reason to conclude that God has reopened
contact with man for revelation in our modern day
(Deu 4:2).

It is also my opinion that the list of New Testament

gifts is exhaustive. That is not to say that each one is defined in such specificity that we are required to understand it today only in its first-century sense. For example, the exercise of the gift of helps in 1975 may extend to scores of different ways of carrying out a ministry to other people within the congregation. Many of these ways would have been impossible in the first century, given the capacities and capabilities of a local church.

On the other hand, I *am* taking issue with Mains when he talks about the gifts listed in the New Testament as being "illustrations."

> If an all-inclusive catalog of gifts had been intended, I believe these passages would contain identical listings, especially since they are written by the same author. Just as I believe the various aspects of the fruit of the spirit as identified in Galatians 5 (love, joy, peace, etc.) are representative—that is, the writer does not intend to include every possible virtuous quality—so the scriptural gifts of the Holy Spirit are to be understood in a similar way. Therefore it seems obvious to me that there are gifts not included in the New Testament listings, such as music, writing, painting, dramatics, etc.[2]

It occurs to me that this kind of suggestion leaves us open to playing fast and loose with the text of Scripture. It also seems to cloud any distinction between spiritual gifts and natural talents.

2. No gift is precluded from appearance today, should the Holy Spirit's sovereignty so design.

This is, of course, the big debate of the seventies. One way to rid the Church of the abuse of certain spiritual gifts is simply to say that they do not exist today, and whatever one has when he claims one of these "temporary gifts" must be explained in some other way. I rather agree with Snyder that "such a position arbitrarily limits the operation of the Holy Spirit and the applicability of the New Testament to our day. There is no more warrant,

for instance, to apply chapters twelve and fourteen of
First Corinthians exclusively to the early Church than
there is so to limit the thirteenth chapter. Gifts and love
go together."[3]

Again, there is no demand that a gift in any other age
took the same form which it had during the days of the
early Church. Nor does it seem to be necessary that gifts
always be linked with offices as was more common in the
first century.

3. *No gift is required of or given to all believers.* The
very significance of the sovereignty of the Holy Spirit in
giving spiritual gifts is at stake here. If we can judge a
Christian's spirituality by whether or not he has received
a certain gift, we will soon have divided ourselves into
the "haves" and "have nots," which was precisely the
problem of carnality in the Corinthian congregation.

By the same token, no gift may be commanded from
God. After clearly indicating in a series of rhetorical
questions that no gift is normative of every Christian
(1 Co 12:29-30), Paul goes on to suggest that we may
make efforts toward having the more useful gifts. I pre-
sume this would allow praying for certain gifts, but never
with the attitude that God "owes us" those gifts just
because we have asked Him for them.

4. *No gift marks believers as uniquely spiritual or
special.* Where a New Testament gift was closely correlated
with an office, there was a distinction (the gift of pastoral
ministry would be an example), and the contribution
which a spiritual gift makes to the edification of the Body
seems to be the basic criterion upon which it is judged
in quality. However, who receives what gift to make
what contribution to the Body is the prerogative of the
Holy Spirit alone, and the only proper response is a
humble recognition of how God's grace is operative in
the whole process.

1. *All gifts are related to the Body, its upbuilding, and
its ministry.* Not everyone must use his spiritual gift only

within the walls of a church building. When Paul talks about "the body," he is talking about the universal Church. Of course we experience the universal Church in a practical manner through given local churches in space and time relationships. The gift of evangelism may operate in the world, but its ultimate benefit is to the universal Church. The gift of teaching may be exercised through child evangelism or a campus Bible class under the sponsorship of the Navigators or IVCF, but the benefit accrues to the Body of Christ.

2. *All gifts represent supernatural levels of more common ministries.* For example, every Christian is responsible to witness, but there is a gift of evangelism. Every Christian is responsible for teaching to some extent, but there is a specific gift of teaching. Every Christian can speak a word of comfort to his neighbor, but there is a gift of exhortation. Every Christian should participate in proportionate giving of his income, but there is a gift of giving.

Spiritual gifts are supernatural because they operate within a supernatural entity, they are given from a supernatural source, and they operate on the basis of a supernatural power. This is precisely the difference between serving Christ in the flesh (or trying to do so) and serving Him properly within the sphere of the Spirit's filling in our lives.

3. *All gifts are to be exercised in humility, unity, and love.* The unique location of 1 Corinthians 13, coming as it does between the content of chapter 12 and that of chapter 14, highlights the necessity of *agape* in the exercise of spiritual gifts. No spiritual gift is of any merit whatsoever if it is not exercised in love. In addition to the dynamic of 1 Corinthians 13, we have Peter's words: "Most important of all, continue to show deep love for each other, for love makes up for many of your faults" (1 Pe 4:8, TLB).

4. *All gifts are geared to personal ministry.* To state it

even more clearly, one might say all gifts have to do with the way we serve other people. One teaches *people;* one helps *people;* one leads *people.* Being the Church is recognizing the constant mutuality of relationship which is ours. Like everything else the Christian has, his spiritual gift does not belong to him. It is Christ's, and he is a steward of its use.

Perhaps no better words can be spoken to conclude a study of the spiritual gifts than those which Peter has already written in his treatment of the subject:

> God has given each of you some special abilities; be sure to use them to help each other, passing on to others God's many kinds of blessings. Are you called to preach? Then preach as though God himself were speaking through you. Are you called to help others? Do it with all the strength and energy that God supplies, so that God will be glorified through Jesus Christ—to him be glory and power forever and ever. Amen (1 Pe 4:10-11, TLB).

NOTES

Introduction

1. J. H. Thayer, *A Greek-English Lexicon of the New Testament* (New York: American Book, 1886), p. 667.
2. Charles C. Ryrie, *The Holy Spirit* (Chicago: Moody, 1965), p. 83.
3. Thomas C. Edwards, *A Commentary on the First Epistle to the Corinthians* (London: Hodder & Stoughton, 1903), p. 312.
4. Joseph A. Beet, *A Commentary on St. Paul's Epistles to the Corinthians* (London: Hodder & Stoughton, 1892), p. 215.
5. Edwards, p. 314.
6. Theodore H. Epp, *The Other Comforter* (Lincoln, Nebr.: Back to the Bible, 1966), pp. 81-91.
7. Ryrie, pp. 83-91.
8. John F. Walvoord, *The Holy Spirit* (Findlay, O.: Dunham, 1958), pp. 168-88.
9. Ray C. Stedman, *Body Life* (Glendale, Calif.: Regal, 1972), p. 40.
10. Stedman, "Equipped for Community," *His*, Mar. 1972, p. 3.
11. Walvoord, p. 166.

1

1. Gerhard Kittel, ed., *Theological Dictionary of the New Testament* (Grand Rapids: Eerdmans, 1968), 3:1036.
2. Archibald Robertson and Alfred Plummer, *A Critical and Exegetical Commentary on the First Epistle of Paul to the Corinthians*, The International Critical Commentary (New York: Scribner's, 1911), p. 281.
3. Albert Barnes, *Notes on the New Testament: 1 Corinthians* (Grand Rapids: Baker, 1949), p. 278.
4. Thomas C. Edwards, *A Commentary on the First Epistle to the Corinthians*, p. 335.

2

1. F. Godet, *Commentary on St. Paul's First Epistle to the Corinthians* (Edinburgh: T. & T. Clark, 1898), 2:225.
2. John Peter Lange, "Ephesians," *A Commentary on the Holy Scriptures*, Vol. 21 (Grand Rapids: Zondervan, n.d.), p. 149.

3

1. A. T. Robertson, *Word Pictures in the New Testament* (Nashville, Tenn.: Broadman, 1931), 4:169.
2. Thomas C. Edwards, *A Commentary on the First Epistle to the Corinthians*, p. 318.
3. *Newsweek*, Apr. 9, 1973, p. 41.

4

1. As quoted in Francis Foulkes, *The Epistle of Paul to the Ephesians* (Grand Rapids: Eerdmans, 1963), p. 119.
2. John F. Walvoord, *The Holy Spirit*, p. 170.
3. John MacPherson, *Commentary on St. Paul's Epistle to the Ephesians* (Edinburgh: T. & T. Clark, 1892), p. 309.

5

1. C. E. B. Cranfield, *A Commentary on the Holy Scriptures* (London: Oliver & Boyd, 1965), p. 33.
2. Martin Luther, *Lectures on Romans*, The Library of Christian Classics, 5:336.
3. Albert Barnes, *Notes on the New Testament: Romans*, p. 278.

6

1. A. T. Robertson, *Word Pictures in the New Testament*, 4:169.

7

1. R. C. H. Lenski, *The Interpretation of St. Paul's Epistle to the Romans* (Columbus, O.: Wartburg, 1945), p. 764.
2. W. H. Griffith Thomas, *Romans—A Devotional Commentary* (London: Religious Tract Society, 1912), p. 26.
3. F. Godet, *Commentary on the Epistle to the Romans* (Grand Rapids: Zondervan, 1956; reprinted from 1883), pp. 432-33.

8

1. Gerhard Kittel, ed., *Theological Dictionary of the New Testament*, 3:213-14.
2. Don W. Hillis, *Tongues, Healing, and You* (Grand Rapids: Baker, 1969), Part II, p. 9.
3. Ray C. Stedman, *Body Life*, p. 43.
4. John F. Walvoord, *The Holy Spirit*, p. 180.
5. Stedman, p. 44.
6. Alan Redpath, *The Royal Route to Heaven* (Westwood, N. J.: Revell, 1960), p. 142.
7. "Healing in the Spirit," *Christianity Today*, July 20, 1973, p. 9.

9

1. John Peter Lange, *A Commentary on the Holy Scriptures*, 20: 253.
2. Archibald Robertson and Alfred Plummer, *A Critical and Exegetical Commentary on the First Epistle of Paul to the Corinthians*, The International Critical Commentary, p. 268.
3. Charles R. Smith, *Tongues in Biblical Perspective* (Winona Lake, Ind.: BMH Books, 1972), p. 99.

10

1. John Peter Lange, *A Commentary on the Holy Scriptures*, 20: 251.
2. Thomas C. Edwards, *A Commentary on the First Epistle to the Corinthians*, p. 315.
3. Joseph A. Beet, *A Commentary on St. Paul's Epistles to the Corinthians*, p. 215.
4. F. Godet, *Commentary on St. Paul's First Epistle to the Corinthians*, 2:195.
5. John Calvin, *Commentaries on the Epistle to the Corinthians* trans. John Pringle (Edinburgh: Calvin Translation Society 1947), 1:40.
6. A. T. Robertson, *Word Pictures in the New Testament*, 4:169
7. Godet, p. 196.

11

1. F. Godet, *Commentary on St. Paul's Epistle to the Romans* 2:293.
2. John H. McClanahan, "Helping When There's a Cry for Help," *Church Administration*, Sept. 1973, p. 6.
3. Matthew Henry, *Matthew Henry's Commentary on the Whole Bible* (New York: Revell, n.d.), 6:461.
4. C. E. B. Cranfield, *A Commentary on the Holy Scriptures*, p 36.
5. Siegfried Grossman, *There Are Other Gifts Than Tongues* (Wheaton, Ill.: Tyndale, 1973), p. 27.

12

1. Gerhard Kittel, ed., *Theological Dictionary of the New Testament*, 1:376.
2. Ibid., 2:87.
3. W. G. T. Shedd, *Commentary on Romans* (New York: Scribner's, 1879), p. 364.
4. C. E. B. Cranfield, *A Commentary on the Holy Scriptures*, p 32.

13

. F. Godet, *Commentary on St. Paul's First Epistle to the Corinthians*, 2:226.

14

. Francis Foulkes, *The Epistle of Paul to the Ephesians*, p. 119.
. John Peter Lange, "Ephesians," *A Commentary on the Holy Scriptures*, Vol. 21, p. 150.
. David R. Mains, *Full Circle* (Waco, Tex.: Word, 1971), p. 68.

15

. Gerhard Kittel, ed., *Theological Dictionary of the New Testament*, 6:830.
. A. T. Robertson, *Word Pictures in the New Testament*, 4:403.

16

. Howard A. Snyder, "Misunderstanding Spiritual Gifts," *Christianity Today*, Oct. 12, 1973, pp. 15-16.
. John MacPherson, *Commentary on St. Paul's Epistle to the Ephesians*, p. 311.
. Gerhard Kittel, ed., *Theological Dictionary of the New Testament*, 2:152.
. W. G. T. Shedd, *Commentary on Romans*, p. 364.
. Archibald Robertson and Alfred Plummer, *A Critical and Exegetical Commentary on the First Epistle of Paul to the Corinthians*, The International Critical Commentary, pp. 279-80.
. Roy B. Zuck, *The Holy Spirit in Your Teaching* (Wheaton, Ill.: Scripture Press, 1963), p. 74.

17

. Kenneth S. Kantzer, "The Tongues Movement of Today: Bane or Blessing," *Trinity Today*, Oct. 1971, p. 6.
. Charles R. Smith, *Tongues in Biblical Perspective* (Winona Lake, Ind.: BMH Books, 1972), p. 40.
. John F. Walvoord, *The Holy Spirit*, p. 182.
. Gerhard Kittel, ed., *Theological Dictionary of the New Testament*, 1:722.
. Stanley N. Gundry, "Facing the Issue of Tongues," *Moody Monthly*, Oct. 1973, p. 100.
. William J. Samarin, *Tongues of Men and Angels* (New York: Macmillan, 1972).
. Ray Stedman, *Body Life*, p. 47.
. Charles C. Ryrie, *The Holy Spirit*, p. 89.
. Smith, p. 92.

10. Gundry, p. 101.
11. Clark H. Pinnock, "The New Pentecostalism: Reflections by a Well-Wisher," *Christianity Today*, Sept. 14, 1973, p. 8.
12. Millard J. Erickson, "Is Tongues-Speaking for Today?" *The Standard*, Nov. 1, 1973, p. 21.

18

1. Thomas C. Edwards, *A Commentary on the First Epistle to the Corinthians*, p. 315.
2. F. Godet, *Commentary on St. Paul's First Epistle to the Corinthians*, 2:195-96.
3. Archibald Robertson and Alfred Plummer, *A Critical and Exegetical Commentary on the First Epistle of Paul to the Corinthians*, The International Critical Commentary, p. 265.

Conclusion

1. Ray Stedman, "Equipped for Community," *His*, p. 3.
2. David R. Mains, *Full Circle*, p. 60.
3. Howard A. Snyder, "Misunderstanding Spiritual Gifts," *Christianity Today*, p. 15.